SPECTRUM

Test Prep

Grade 7

D1317597

Mc Graw Hill **McGraw-Hill**
Children's Publishing

Columbus, Ohio

Credits:
McGraw-Hill Children's Publishing Editorial/Art & Design Team
Vincent F. Douglas, *President*
Tracey E. Dils, *Publisher*
Phyllis Sibbing, B.S. Ed., *Project Editor*
Rose Audette, *Art Director*

Also Thanks to:
MaryAnne Nestor, Layout and Production
Jenny Campbell, Interior Illustration

McGraw-Hill
Children's Publishing
A Division of The **McGraw·Hill** Companies

Published by American Education Publishing, an imprint of McGraw-Hill Children's Publishing
Copyright © 2002 McGraw-Hill Children's Publishing.

Send all inquiries to:
McGraw-Hill Children's Publishing
8787 Orion Place
Columbus, OH 43240-4027

ISBN 1-57768-667-5

2 3 4 5 6 7 8 9 VHG 07 06 05 04 03 02

Table of Contents

Just for Parents

About the Tests 4
How to Help Your Child Prepare for Standardized Testing 8

For All Students

Taking Standardized Tests 10
Terms to Know 14
Skills Checklist 16
Preparing All Year Round 20
Homework Log and Weekly Schedule 22
What's Ahead in This Book? 24

Kinds of Questions

Multiple Choice Questions 25
Fill-in-the-Blank Questions 27
True/False Questions 29
Matching Questions 31
Analogy Questions 33
Short Answer Questions 35

Subject Help

Reading 37
Language Arts 39
Mathematics 45
Social Studies 65
Science 70

Practice Test and Final Test

Introduction 73
Table of Contents 74
Name Sheet 75
Record Your Scores 76
Practice Test Answer Sheet 77
Practice Test 79
Final Test Answer Sheet 123
Final Test 125
Answer Key 153

About the Tests

What Are Standardized Achievement Tests?

Achievement tests measure what children know in particular subject areas such as reading, language arts, and mathematics. They do not measure your child's intelligence or ability to learn.

When tests are standardized, or *normed,* children's test results are compared with those of a specific group who have taken the test, usually at the same age or grade.

Standardized achievement tests measure what children around the country are learning. The test makers survey popular textbook series, as well as state curriculum frameworks and other professional sources, to determine what content is covered widely.

Because of variations in state frameworks and textbook series, as well as grade ranges on some test levels, the tests may cover some material that children have not yet learned. This is especially true if the test is offered early in the school year. However, test scores are compared to those of other children who take the test at the same time of year, so your child will not be at a disadvantage if his or her class has not covered specific material yet.

Different School Districts, Different Tests

There are many flexible options for districts when offering standardized tests. Many school districts choose not to give the full test battery, but select certain content and scoring options. For example, many schools may test only in the areas of reading and mathematics. Similarly, a state or district may use one test for certain grades and another test for other grades. These decisions are often based on

the amount of time and money a district wishes to spend on test administration. Some states choose to develop their own statewide assessment tests.

On pages 5, 6, and 7 you will find information about these five widely used standardized achievement tests:

- California Achievement Tests (CAT)
- Terra Nova/CTBS
- Iowa Test of Basic Skills (ITBS)
- Stanford Achievement Test (SAT9)
- Metropolitan Achievement Test (MAT).

However, this book contains strategies and practice questions for use with a variety of tests. Even if your state does not give one of the five tests listed above, your child will benefit from doing the practice questions in this book. If you're unsure about which test your child takes, contact your local school district to find out which tests are given.

Types of Test Questions

Traditionally, standardized achievements tests have used only multiple choice questions. Today, many tests may include constructed response (short answer) and extended response (essay) questions as well.

In addition, many tests include questions that tap students' higher-order thinking skills. Instead of simple recall questions, such as identifying a date in history, questions may require students to make comparisons and contrasts or analyze results, among other skills.

What the Tests Measure

These tests do not measure your child's level of intelligence, but they do show how well your child knows material that he or she has learned and that is also covered on the tests. It's important to remember that some tests cover content that is not taught in your child's school or grade. In other instances, depending on when in the year the test is given, your child may not yet have covered the material.

If the test reports you receive show that your child needs improvement in one or more skill areas, you may want to seek help from your child's teacher and find out how you can work with your child to improve his or her skills.

California Achievement Tests (CAT/5)

What Is the *California Achievement Test*?

The *California Achievement Test* is a standardized achievement test battery that is widely used with elementary through high school students.

Parts of the Test

The CAT includes tests in the following content areas:

Reading
- Word Analysis
- Vocabulary
- Comprehension

Spelling

Language Arts
- Language Mechanics
- Language Usage

Mathematics

Science

Social Studies

Your child may take some or all of these subtests if your district uses the *California Achievement Test*.

Terra Nova/CTBS (Comprehensive Tests of Basic Skills)

What Is the *Terra Nova/CTBS*?

The *Terra Nova/Comprehensive Tests of Basic Skills* is a standardized achievement test battery used in elementary through high school grades.

While many of the test questions on the *Terra Nova* are in the traditional multiple choice form, your child may take parts of the *Terra Nova* that include some open-ended questions (constructed-response items).

Parts of the Test

Your child may take some or all of the following subtests if your district uses the *Terra Nova/CTBS*:

Reading/Language Arts
Mathematics
Science
Social Studies

Supplementary tests include:
- Word Analysis
- Vocabulary
- Language Mechanics
- Spelling
- Mathematics Computation

Critical thinking skills may also be tested.

Iowa Tests of Basic Skills (ITBS)

What Is the *ITBS*?

The *Iowa Test of Basic Skills* is a standardized achievement test battery used in elementary through high school grades.

Parts of the Test

Your child may take some or all of these subtests if your district uses the *ITBS*, also known as the *Iowa*:

Reading
- Vocabulary
- Reading Comprehension

Language Arts
- Spelling
- Capitalization
- Punctuation
- Usage and Expression

Math
- Concepts/Estimate
- Problems/Data Interpretation

Social Studies
Science
Sources of Information

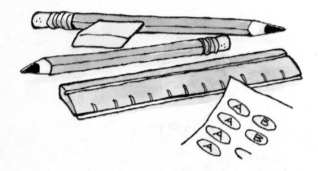

Stanford Achievement Test (SAT9)

What Is the *Stanford Achievement Test*?

The *Stanford Achievement Test, Ninth Edition (SAT9)* is a standardized achievement test battery used in elementary through high school grades.

Note that the *Stanford Achievement Test (SAT9)* is a different test from the *SAT* used by high school students for college admissions.

While many of the test questions on the *SAT9* are in traditional multiple choice form, your child may take parts of the *SAT9* that include some open-ended questions (constructed-response items).

Parts of the Test

Your child may take some or all of these subtests if your district uses the *Stanford Achievement Test*:

Reading
- Vocabulary
- Reading Comprehension

Mathematics
- Problem Solving
- Procedures

Language Arts
Spelling
Study Skills
Listening
Critical thinking skills may also be tested.

Metropolitan Achievement Test (MAT7 and MAT8)

What Is the *Metropolitan Achievement Test*?

The *Metropolitan Achievement Test* is a standardized achievement test battery used in elementary through high school grades.

Parts of the Test

Your child may take some or all of these subtests if your district uses the *Metropolitan Achievement Test*:

Reading
- Vocabulary
- Reading Comprehension

Math
- Concepts and Problem Solving
- Computation

Language Arts
- Pre-writing
- Composing
- Editing

Science
Social studies
Research skills
Thinking skills
Spelling

Statewide Assessments

Today the majority of states give statewide assessments. In some cases these tests are known as *high-stakes assessments*. This means that students must score at a certain level in order to be promoted. Some states use minimum competency or proficiency tests. Often these tests measure more basic skills than other types of statewide assessments.

Statewide assessments are generally linked to state curriculum frameworks. Frameworks provide a blueprint, or outline, to ensure that teachers are covering the same curriculum topics as other teachers in the same grade level in the state. In some states, standardized achievement tests (such as the five described in this book) are used in connection with statewide assessments.

When Statewide Assessments Are Given

Statewide assessments may not be given at every grade level. Generally, they are offered at one or more grades in elementary school, middle school, and high school. Many states test at grades 4, 8, and 10.

State-by-State Information

You can find information about statewide assessments and curriculum frameworks at your state Department of Education Web site. To find the address for your individual state go to www.ed.gov, click on Topics A–Z, and then click on State Departments of Education. You will find a list of all the state departments of education, mailing addresses, and Web sites.

How to Help Your Child Prepare for Standardized Testing

Preparing All Year Round

Perhaps the most valuable way you can help your child prepare for standardized achievement tests is by providing enriching experiences. Keep in mind also, that test results for younger children are not as reliable as for older students. If a child is hungry, tired, or upset, this may result in a poor test score. Here are some tips on how you can help your child do his or her best on standardized tests.

Read aloud with your child. Reading aloud helps develop vocabulary and fosters a positive attitude toward reading. Reading together is one of the most effective ways you can help your child succeed in school.

Share experiences. Baking cookies together, planting a garden, or making a map of your neighborhood are examples of activities that help build skills that are measured on the tests such as sequencing and following directions.

Become informed about your state's testing procedures. Ask about or watch for announcements of meetings that explain about standardized tests and statewide assessments in your school district.

Talk to your child's teacher about your child's individual performance on these state tests during a parent-teacher conference.

Help your child know what to expect. Read and discuss with your child the test-taking tips in this book. Your child can prepare by working through a couple of strategies a day so that no practice session takes too long.

Help your child with his or her regular school assignments. Set up a quiet study area for homework. Supply this area with pencils, paper, markers, a calculator, a ruler, a dictionary, scissors, glue, and so on. Check your child's homework and offer to help if he or she gets stuck. But remember, it's your child's homework, not yours. If you help too much, your child will not benefit from the activity.

Keep in regular contact with your child's teacher. Attend parent-teacher conferences, school functions, PTA or PTO meetings, and school board meetings. This will help you get to know the educators in your district and the families of your child's classmates.

Learn to use computers as an educational resource. If you do not have a computer and Internet access at home, try your local library.

Remember—simply getting your child comfortable with testing procedures and helping him or her know what to expect can improve test scores!

Getting Ready for the Big Day

There are lots of things you can do on or immediately before test day to improve your child's chances of testing success. What's more, these strategies will help your child prepare him or herself for school tests, too, and promote general study skills that can last a lifetime.

Provide a good breakfast on test day. Instead of sugar cereal, which provides immediate but not long-term energy, have your child eat a breakfast with protein or complex carbohydrates such as an egg, whole grain cereal or toast, or a banana-yogurt shake.

Promote a good night's sleep. A good night's sleep before the test is essential. Try not to overstress the importance of the test. This may cause your child to lose sleep because of anxiety. Doing some exercise after school and having a quiet evening routine will help your child sleep well the night before the test.

Assure your child that he or she is not expected to know all of the answers on the test. Explain that other children in higher grades may take the same test, and that the test may measure things your child has not yet learned in school. Help your child understand that you expect him or her to put forth a good effort—and that this is enough. Your child should not try to cram for these tests. Also avoid threats or bribes; these put undue pressure on children and may interfere with their best performance.

Keep the mood light and offer encouragement. To provide a break on test days, do something fun and special after school—take a walk around the neighborhood, play a game, read a favorite book, or prepare a special snack together. These activities keep your child's mood light—even if the testing sessions have been difficult—and show how much you appreciate your child's effort.

Taking Standardized Tests

No matter what grade you're in, this is information you can use to prepare for standardized tests. Here is what you'll find:

- Test-taking tips and strategies to use on test day and year-round.
- Important terms to know for Language Arts, Reading, Math, Science, and Social Studies.
- A checklist of skills to complete to help you understand what you need to know in Language Arts, Reading Comprehension, Writing, and Math.
- General study/homework tips.

By opening this book, you've already taken your first step towards test success. The rest is easy—all you have to do is get started!

What You Need to Know

There are many things you can do to increase your test success. Here's a list of tips to keep in mind when you take standardized tests—and when you study for them, too.

Keep up with your school work. One way you can succeed in school and on tests is by studying and doing your homework regularly. Studies show that you remember only about one-fifth of what you memorize the night before a test. That's one good reason not to try to learn it all at once! Keeping up with your work throughout the year will help you remember the material better. You also won't be as tired or nervous as if you try to learn everything at once.

Feel your best. One of the ways you can do your best on tests and in school is to make sure your body is ready. To do this, get a good night's sleep each night and eat a healthy breakfast (not sugary cereal that will leave you tired by the middle of the morning). An egg or a milkshake with yogurt and fresh fruit will give you lasting energy. Also, wear comfortable clothes, maybe your lucky shirt or your favorite color on test day. It can't hurt, and it may even help you relax.

Be prepared. Do practice questions and learn about how standardized tests are organized. Books like this one will help you know what to expect when you take a standardized test.

When you are taking the test, follow the directions. It is important to listen carefully to the directions your teacher gives and to read the written instructions carefully. Words like *not*, *none*, *rarely*, *never*, and *always* are very important in test directions and questions. You may want to circle words like these.

Look at each page carefully before you start answering. In school you usually read a passage and then answer questions about it. But when you take a test, it's helpful to follow a different order.

If you are taking a Reading test, first read the directions. Then read the *questions* before you read the passage. This way you will know exactly what kind of information to look for as you read. Next, read the passage carefully. Finally, answer the questions.

On math and science tests, look at the labels on graphs and charts. Think about what each graph or chart shows. Questions often will ask you to draw conclusions about the information.

Manage your time. *Time management* means using your time wisely on a test so that you can finish as much of it as possible and do your best. Look over the test or the parts that you are allowed to do at one time. Sometimes you may want to do the easier parts first. This way, if you run out of time before you finish, you will have completed a good chunk of the work.

For tests that have a time limit, notice what time it is when the test begins and figure out when you need to stop. Check a few times as you work through the test to be sure you are making good progress and not spending too much time on any particular section.

You don't have to keep up with everyone else. You may notice other students in the class finishing before you do. Don't worry about this. Everyone works at a different pace. Just keep going, trying not to spend too long on any one question.

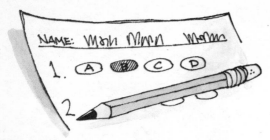

Fill in answer circles properly. Even if you know every answer on a test, you won't do well unless you enter the answers correctly on the answer sheet.

Fill in the entire circle, but don't spend too much time making it perfect. Make your mark dark, but not so dark that it goes through the paper! And be sure you only choose one answer for each question, even if you are not sure. If you choose two answers, both will be marked as wrong.

It's usually not a good idea to change your answers. Usually your first choice is the right one. Unless you realize that you misread the question, the directions, or some facts in a passage, it's usually safer to stay with your first answer. If you are pretty sure it's wrong, of course, go ahead and change it. Make sure you completely erase the first choice and neatly fill in your new choice.

Use context clues to figure out tough questions. If you come across a word or idea you don't understand, use context clues—the words in the sentences nearby— to help you figure out its meaning.

Sometimes it's good to guess. Should you guess when you don't know an answer on a test? That depends. If your teacher has made the test, usually you will score better if you answer as many questions as possible, even if you don't really know the answers.

On standardized tests, here's what to do to score your best. For each question, most of these tests let you choose from four or five answer choices. If you decide that a couple of answers are clearly wrong but you're still not sure about the answer, go ahead and make your best guess. If you can't narrow down the choices at all, then you may be better off skipping the question. Tests like these take away extra points for wrong answers, so it's better to leave them blank. Be sure you skip over the answer space for these questions on the answer sheet, though, so you don't fill in the wrong spaces.

Sometimes you should skip a question and come back to it.

On many tests, you will score better if you answer more questions. This means that you should not spend too much time on any single question. Sometimes it gets tricky, though, keeping track of questions you skipped on your answer sheet.

If you want to skip a question because you don't know the answer, put a very light pencil mark next to the question in the test booklet. Try to choose an answer, even if you're not sure of it. Fill in the answer lightly on the answer sheet.

Check your work. On a standardized test, you can't go ahead or skip back to another section of the test. But you may go back and review your answers on the section you just worked on if you have extra time.

First, scan your answer sheet. Make sure that you answered every question you could. Also, if you are using a bubble-type answer sheet, make sure that you filled in only one bubble for each question. Erase any extra marks on the page.

Finally—avoid test anxiety! If you get nervous about tests, don't worry. *Test anxiety* happens to lots of good students. Being a little nervous actually sharpens your mind. But if you get very nervous about tests, take a few minutes to relax the night before or the day of the test. One good way to relax is to get some exercise, even if you just have time to stretch, shake out your fingers, and wiggle your toes. If you can't move around, it helps just to take a few slow, deep breaths and picture yourself doing a great job!

Terms to Know

Here's a list of terms that are good to know when taking standardized tests. Don't be worried if you see something new. You may not have learned it in school yet.

acute angle an angle of less than 90 degrees

area the amount of surface within a flat shape

atom the smallest part of an element that still has all the properties of that element

chemical change a permanent change to a substance in which the chemical composition of that substance is also changed

circumference the distance around a circle

compass rose a small icon which shows where north, south, east, and west are on a map

conclusion in science, a judgment made after evaluating data from an experiment or body of information

consumer an organism that cannot make its own food and therefore must consume matter produced by other organisms

coordinates numbers that show the location of a given point on a graph, map, or line

decomposer an organism that breaks plant and animal matter down into smaller parts

delta a triangle-shaped area of land at the base of a river where sand or mud collects

diameter the distance across a circle at its widest point

direct object in a sentence, the person or thing that receives the action of a verb

ecosystem a group of animals and plants living together and interacting with their environment

equator the imaginary line that divides the Earth in half exactly between the North and South poles

factor a whole number that can be divided into a larger number without remainder

genre a category of literature

hypothesis a testable prediction about the outcome of an experiment

integer any whole number, positive or negative

latitude the location of a specific place, measured in degrees north or south of the equator

longitude the location of a specific place, measured in degrees east or west of the prime meridian

metaphor a way of describing one thing by calling it something else

obtuse angle an angle larger than 90 degrees but less than 180 degrees

parallel what two straight lines are if they are the same distance from one another at every point and never meet

peninsula a landform that juts out from a larger body of land and is almost entirely surrounded by water

perimeter the distance around a shape or object

perpendicular a line that creates right angles as it intersects with another line

personification giving human-like properties to something that is not human

physical change a reversible change to a substance in which the chemical composition of that substance stays the same

plateau an area of high, flat land surrounded by lower land or water

polygon a closed, flat shape with at least three straight sides

predicate the part of a sentence that tells what the subject did or was done to the subject

prediction a guess about the outcome of an event

prefix a group of letters added to the beginning of a word or root to change its meaning

prime meridian the imaginary line of longitude, passing through Greenwich, England, from which all other longitude is measured

prime number a number with exactly two factors

probability the likelihood that an event will happen

producer an organism which is capable of producing its own food from nonliving materials, just as plants make their own food from the sun's light

pronoun a word that takes the place of a noun

quotient the result of dividing one number by another

radius the distance from the center of a circle to any point along its outer edge

ratio a comparison of two quantities, often shown as a fraction

ray a piece of a line that starts at a given point and extends infinitely in one direction

right angle an angle of exactly 90 degrees

savanna a flat area of land, covered with grass but few trees

scale an icon which shows the ratio of distance on a map to distance in real life

segment part of a line with definite ending and starting points

simile a description that tells about one thing by comparing it to something else, using *like* or *as*

square root the factor of a number which, when multiplied by itself, results in that number

subject in a sentence, the words that tell who or what the sentence is about

suffix a group of letters added to the end of a word or root to change its meaning

symmetry when an object or shape, divided exactly in half down the middle, has matching parts on both sides

Skills Checklist

Which subjects do you need more practice in? Use these checklists to find out. Put a check mark next to each statement that is true for you. Then use the unchecked statements to figure out which skills you need to review.

Keep in mind that if you are using these checklists in the middle of the school year, you may not have learned some skills yet. Talk to your teacher or a parent if you need help with a new skill.

Reading

☐ I can use context clues to figure out tough words.

☐ I know what synonyms are and how to use them.

☐ I know what antonyms are and how to use them.

☐ I can find words with opposite meanings.

☐ I can tell the difference between a fact and an opinion.

☐ I know the different genres of writing (fiction, nonfiction, etc.)

☐ I can predict what will happen next in a story.

☐ I can paraphrase and summarize what I read.

☐ I can compare and contrast characters and events.

☐ I can rephrase the main idea in a sentence or paragraph.

☐ I can recognize the author's purpose for writing.

☐ I can choose the correct topic sentence for a paragraph

Language Arts

I can identify the different parts of speech.

☐ subject and object pronouns

☐ direct and indirect objects

☐ prepositions

☐ verbs

☐ verb tenses (past, present, and future)

☐ linking verbs

☐ adjectives

☐ adverbs

☐ conjunctions

☐ prefixes and suffixes

I know how to

- [ ] form negatives correctly.

- [ ] choose the best way to write a sentence.

- [ ] identify complete and incomplete sentences.

- [ ] identify run-on sentences.

- [ ] combine sentences.

- [ ] identify the different parts of a sentence.

- [ ] identify correctly spelled words.

- [ ] identify correct capitalization of words.

- [ ] identify correct punctuation.

Writing

Before I write

- [ ] I think about my purpose for writing (to persuade, inform, entertain, describe, etc.).

- [ ] I brainstorm ideas to include in my writing.

When I write a draft

- [ ] I use paragraphs that contain a main idea and supporting details.

- [ ] I use dialogue, action, and descriptive words to tell about my characters.

- [ ] I include details that tell about the setting.

- [ ] I write in different genres.

- [ ] I use reference materials (encyclopedias, dictionaries, the Internet) to find information.

- [ ] I use cause and effect, sequence of events, and other systems to organize my writing.

As I revise my work

- [ ] I check for spelling, capitalization, punctuation, and grammar mistakes.

- [ ] I make sure my paragraphs are well-organized.

- [ ] I add descriptive words and sentences to make my work more interesting.

- [ ] I neatly write or type my final copy.

- [ ] I include my name and a title on the finished work.

Mathematics

Number Sense

I can

- [ ] identify the multiples of a number.
- [ ] find averages.
- [ ] use roman numerals.

Multiplication and Division

I can

- [ ] multiply three-digit numbers and greater.
- [ ] divide three-digit numbers and greater.
- [ ] multiply and divide by decimals.
- [ ] multiply and divide by powers of 10.
- [ ] multiply negative numbers.

Measurement

I can estimate and measure using the standard units for

- [ ] length (inch, foot, yard, mile).
- [ ] weight (ounce, pound, ton).
- [ ] capacity (cup, pint, quart, gallon).
- [ ] time (seconds, minutes, hours).

I can estimate and measure using the metric units for

- [ ] length (centimeter, decimeter, meter, kilometer).
- [ ] mass (gram, kilogram).
- [ ] capacity (milliliter, liter).
- [ ] I can solve simple problems with units of time, length, weight/mass, capacity, and temperature.

Fractions and Decimals

I can

- [ ] compare and order fractions.
- [ ] use the least common multiple.
- [ ] find prime and common factors.
- [ ] add and subtract fractions and mixed numbers.
- [ ] multiply and divide fractions, mixed numbers, decimals, and integers.
- [ ] use ratios and proportions.
- [ ] find percentages.

Geometry

I can identify

- ☐ polygons.
- ☐ lines, line segments, and rays.
- ☐ different types of angles, triangles, and quadrilaterals.
- ☐ points on a coordinate system.
- ☐ I can find the perimeter, area, and circumference of shapes.

Algebra

I can

- ☐ use the order of operations.
- ☐ identify the factors of a number.

Problem Solving

I use different strategies to solve different kinds of problems:

- ☐ I estimate and use mental math.
- ☐ I make pictures, diagrams, and charts.
- ☐ I look for patterns.
- ☐ I work backwards.
- ☐ I collect data.
- ☐ I read and construct line graphs, bar graphs, and pie charts.

Preparing All Year Round

Believe it or not, knowing how to study and manage your time is a skill you will use for the rest of your life. There are helpful strategies that you can use to be more successful in school. The following is a list of tips to keep in mind as you study for tests and school assignments.

Get organized. To make it easy to get your homework done, set up a place in which to do it each day. Choose a location where you can give the work your full attention. Find a corner of your room, the kitchen, or another quiet place where you won't be interrupted. Put all the tools you'll need in that area. Set aside a drawer or basket for school supplies. That way you won't have to go hunting each time you need a sharp pencil! Here are some things you may want to keep in your study corner for homework and school projects:

- pencils and pens
- pencil sharpener
- notebook paper
- dictionary
- tape
- glue
- scissors
- stapler
- crayons, markers, colored pencils
- construction paper, printer paper

Schedule your assignments. The best way to keep track of homework and special projects is by planning and managing your time. Keep a schedule of homework assignments and other events to help you get organized. Make your own or make a copy of the **Homework Log and Weekly Schedule** provided on pages 22–23 of this book for each week you're in school.

Record your homework assignments on the log as completely as you can. Enter the book, page number, and exercise number of each assignment. Enter dates of tests as soon as you know them so that you can begin to study ahead of time. Study a section of the material each day. Then review all of it the day before the test.

Also make notes to help you remember special events and materials such as permission slips you need to return. List after-school activities so you can plan your homework and study time around them. Remember to record fun activities on your log, too. You don't want to forget that party you've been invited to or even just time you'd like to spend hanging out or studying with friends.

Do your homework right away. Set aside a special time every day after school to do your homework. You may want to take a break when you first get home, but give yourself plenty of time to do your homework, too. That way you won't get interrupted by dinner or get too tired to finish.

If you are bored or confused by an assignment and you really don't want to do it, promise yourself a little reward, perhaps a snack or 15 minutes of playing ball after you've really worked hard for 45 minutes or so. Then go back to work for a while if you need to, and take another break later.

Get help if you need it. If you need help, just ask. Call a friend or ask a family member for help. If these people can't help you, be sure to ask your teacher the next day about any work you didn't understand.

Use a computer. If you have one available, a computer can be a great tool for doing homework. Typing your homework on the computer lets you hand in neat papers, check your spelling easily, and look up the definitions of words you aren't sure about. If you have an Internet connection, you can also do research without leaving home.

Before you go online, talk with your family about ways to stay safe. Be sure never to give out personal information (your name, age, address, or phone number) without permission.

Practice, practice, practice! The best way to improve your skills in specific subject areas is through lots of practice. If you have trouble in a school subject such as math, science, social studies, language, or reading, doing some extra activities or projects can give you just the boost you need.

Homework Log
and Weekly Schedule

	Monday	Tuesday	Wednesday
MATH			
SOCIAL STUDIES			
SCIENCE			
READING			
LANGUAGE ARTS			
OTHER			

for the week of _____

Thursday	Friday	Saturday / Sunday	
			MATH
			SOCIAL STUDIES
			SCIENCE
			READING
			LANGUAGE ARTS
			OTHER

What's Ahead in This Book?

As you know, you will have to take many tests while in school. But there is no reason to be nervous about taking standardized tests. You can prepare for them by doing your best in school all year. You can also learn about the types of questions you'll see on standardized tests and helpful strategies for answering the questions. That's what this book is all about. It has been developed especially to help you and other seventh graders know what to expect—and what to do—on test day.

The first section will introduce you to the different kinds of questions found on most standardized tests. Multiple choice, short answer, matching, and other types of questions will be explained in detail. You'll get tips for answering each type. Then you'll be given sample questions to work through so you can practice your skills.

Next, you'll find sections on these major school subjects: reading, language arts, math, social studies (sometimes called citizenship), and science. You'll discover traps to watch for in each subject area and tricks you can use to make answering the questions easier. And there are plenty of practice questions provided to sharpen your skills even more.

Finally, you'll find two sections of questions. One is called Practice Test and the other is called Final Test. The questions are designed to look just like the ones you'll be given in school on a real standardized test. An answer key is at the back of the book so you can check your own answers. Once you check your answers, you can see in which subject areas you need more practice.

So good luck—test success is just around the corner!

Multiple Choice Questions

You have probably seen multiple choice questions before. They are the most common type of question used on standardized tests. To answer a multiple choice question, you must choose one answer from a number of choices.

EXAMPLE **Which word does not fit in this group?**
parakeet, heron, _____

Ⓐ cardinal

Ⓑ dove

Ⓒ egret

Ⓓ duck-billed platypus

Sometimes you will know the answer right away. Other times you won't. To answer multiple choice questions on a test, do the following:

Remember

- Read the directions carefully. If you're not sure what you're supposed to do, you might make a lot of mistakes.
- First answer any easy questions whose answers you are sure you know.
- When you come to a harder question, circle the question number. You can come back to this question after you have finished all the easier ones.
- Watch out for clue words like *same, opposite, not, probably, best, most likely,* and *main*. They can change the meaning of a question and/or help you eliminate answer choices.

Words like *same, opposite, not, probably, best, most likely,* and *main* can change the meaning of a question.

Testing It Out

Now look at the sample question more closely.

Think: Let's see: parakeets and herons are birds. I see the word *not*, so I'm looking for a word that is *not* another bird's name. Cardinals and doves are both birds, so **A** and **B** are wrong. I don't know what an egret is, but I do know that a duck-billed platypus is a mammal—not a bird—so I will choose **D**.

Multiple Choice Practice

Directions: Answer questions 1–4. Fill in the circle next to your answer for each one.

1 **Suspicious** is an antonym for ____.

Ⓐ doubtful
Ⓑ trustworthy
Ⓒ dubious
Ⓓ superstition

2 **Migrate** is a synonym for ____.

Ⓕ journey
Ⓖ geese
Ⓗ hibernate
Ⓙ settle

3 Which word fits best in this group?
science fiction, romance ____

Ⓐ alien
Ⓑ movie
Ⓒ comedy
Ⓓ spaceship

4 Which word could not fit in this group? flee, gallop ____

Ⓕ run
Ⓖ walk
Ⓗ hurry
Ⓙ race

Directions: Read the following passage. Then answer the questions below.

Although wolf puppies are cute, they do not make good pets. Wolf puppies grow into 150 pound wild animals that are difficult to control or train. People with wolf puppies are soon faced with a huge dilemma. What's worse, these wolves can't be returned to the wild because they have never learned to hunt for themselves. Fortunately, a number of private groups across the country adopt wolves.

5 The writer's main purpose is to

Ⓐ convince readers not to buy a wolf puppy.
Ⓑ entertain readers with a funny story about wolves.
Ⓒ provide information about wolves.
Ⓓ persuade readers to support groups that adopt wolves.

6 Most people who buy wolf puppies for pets

Ⓕ have thought about what they are doing and decided it is the right thing.
Ⓖ should just let them free when they get tired of them.
Ⓗ are really doing the right thing and should stick it out.
Ⓙ have not given much thought to what happens when they grow up.

Fill-in-the-Blank Questions

On some tests you must fill in something that's missing from a phrase, sentence, equation, or passage.

EXAMPLE   **I was excited because I reached the _____ of the mountain.**

    (A) summer   (C) side

    (B) summit   (D) summary

To answer fill-in-the-blank questions, do the following:

- See if you can think of the answer even before you look at your choices.
- Even if the answer you first thought of is one of the choices, be sure to check the other choices. There may be a better answer.
- Look for the articles *a* and *an* to help you. Since the word *a* must be followed a consonant and *an* is followed by words starting with vowel sounds, you can often use articles to eliminate choices.
- For harder questions, try to fit every answer choice into the blank. Underline clue words that may help you find the correct answer. Write an X after answers that do not fit. Choose the answer that does fit. You can use this strategy to double-check your answers.
- If you get really stuck, try filling in the blank on your own (not choosing from the given answers). Then look for synonyms for your new word/words among the answer choices.

Testing It Out

Now look at the sample question above more closely.

Think: Choice **A**, *summer*, is a season, not a place. That answer doesn't make any sense in this sentence.

Choice **B**, *summit*, makes complete sense; the summit of the mountain is the top. This is probably the answer, but I'll check again.

Side, choice **C**, is also a possibility. "I was excited because I reached the side of the mountain." That could mean something like "I finished a difficult climb."

Choice **D**, *summary*, means "paraphrase." That choice makes no sense in the sentence.

So back to choices **B** and **C**; although *side* might fit in that sentence, *summit* fits better. So the answer must be **B**.

Fill-in-the-Blank Practice

Directions: Find the word that best completes each sentence.
Fill in the circle next to your answer.

1 Ari has been my _____ for 4 years.
- Ⓐ fiend
- Ⓒ fresh
- Ⓑ friend
- Ⓓ brother

2 On Saturday Ari and I _____ to see a play in the park.
- Ⓕ revolved
- Ⓗ resolved
- Ⓖ skipped
- Ⓙ gathering

3 _____, it was canceled because of rain.
- Ⓐ Unfortunately
- Ⓒ Unbelievably
- Ⓑ Impossibly
- Ⓓ Whenever

4 We hurried into a cafe to get out of the _____ storm.
- Ⓕ gruesome
- Ⓗ drizzle
- Ⓖ shocking
- Ⓙ torrential

5 We ordered a pizza and some sodas to _____ our thirst.
- Ⓐ quell
- Ⓒ queue
- Ⓑ quench
- Ⓓ extinguish

6 The _____ coming from the kitchen made our mouths water.
- Ⓕ aroma
- Ⓗ perfume
- Ⓖ odor
- Ⓙ stench

7 Because Ari and I hadn't eaten all day, we were _____ .
- Ⓐ famished
- Ⓒ distraught
- Ⓑ patient
- Ⓓ distracting

8 But the waitress soon _____ our meal.
- Ⓕ withheld
- Ⓗ remembered
- Ⓖ produced
- Ⓙ escorted

9 When we got up to leave, _____.
- Ⓐ The waitress said, I hope you enjoy your meal!
- Ⓑ the waitress said, "i hope you enjoyed your meal!
- Ⓒ The waitress said, I hope you enjoyed your meal!"
- Ⓓ the waitress said, "I hope you enjoyed your meal!"

10 We _____ her that we would come again!
- Ⓕ assured
- Ⓖ assumed
- Ⓗ insured
- Ⓙ asserted

True/False Questions

A true/false question asks you to read a statement and decide if it is right (true) or wrong (false). Sometimes you will be asked to write **T** for true or **F** for false. Most of the time you must fill in a circle for your answer.

EXAMPLE   **Galileo, Copernicus, and Michelangelo were all famous astronomers.**

(A) true

(B) false

To answer true/false questions, do the following:

- First, answer all of the easy questions. Circle the numbers next to harder ones and come back to them later.
- True/false questions with words like *always*, *never*, *all*, *none*, *only*, and *every* are usually false. This is because they limit a statement so much.
- True/false questions with words like *most*, *many*, and *generally* are often true. This is because they make statements more believable.
- Remember that if any part of a statement is false, the entire statement is false.

 **Remember**

True/false questions with words like *always*, *never*, *all*, *none*, *only*, and *every* are usually false.

Testing It Out

Now look at the sample question more closely.

 Think: I remember reading that Galileo made observations of the moon through his telescope. So I know that Galileo was an astronomer. I think that he was a famous astronomer, but I'm not really sure. I've never heard of Copernicus, so I don't know if he was an astronomer or not. But I know that Michelangelo was a famous artist, not an astronomer. So the answer must be **B** for false.

True/False Practice

Directions: Decide if each statement is true or false. Fill in the circle next to your answer.

Galileo Galilei was fascinated by a telescope being sold in the marketplace by a Dutch optician. The new gadget allowed merchants to see ships nearing a harbor.

Using his knowledge of mathematics and optics, Galileo improved upon the Dutch invention. By combining two lenses, one ocular, or close to the eyes, and the other objective, at the other end of the tube, Galileo transformed the telescope into a formidable instrument for astronomical research. With the help of his telescope, Galileo observed the mountains and valleys of the moon, among other heavenly bodies.

1 **Galileo did not invent the telescope.**

Ⓐ true   Ⓑ false

2 **Everyone dreams of traveling to space.**

Ⓐ true   Ⓑ false

3 **Some people use telescopes to look at the moon.**

Ⓐ true   Ⓑ false

4 **The objective lens of the telescope is closer to the eye than the ocular lens.**

Ⓐ true   Ⓑ false

5 **The moon is the only heavenly body in the sky.**

Ⓐ true   Ⓑ false

6 **Generally, a telescope is used for astronomical research.**

Ⓐ true   Ⓑ false

7 **"Astronomy" is the science of looking at the moon.**

Ⓐ true   Ⓑ false

8 **Galileo could see the moon without his telescope.**

Ⓐ true   Ⓑ false

9 **Galileo was the only scientist to observe the moon.**

Ⓐ true   Ⓑ false

10 **In the context above, the word "formidable" means "causing fear."**

Ⓐ true   Ⓑ false

11 **All telescopes are made by Dutch opticians.**

Ⓐ true   Ⓑ false

12 **Galileo used mathematics to improve the telescope.**

Ⓐ true   Ⓑ false

Matching Questions

Matching questions ask you to find pairs of words or phrases that are related in a certain way. The choices are often shown in columns.

EXAMPLE	**Match items that go together.**		
1 photograph	**A** scissors	**1** Ⓐ Ⓑ Ⓒ Ⓓ
2 mural	**B** camera	**2** Ⓐ Ⓑ Ⓒ Ⓓ
3 collage	**C** pencil	**3** Ⓐ Ⓑ Ⓒ Ⓓ
4 cartoon	**D** paintbrush	**4** Ⓐ Ⓑ Ⓒ Ⓓ

When answering matching questions, follow these simple guidelines:

- Begin by figuring out the relationship between the two groups of words.
- When you first look at a matching question, you will probably be able to spot some of the matches right away. So match the easiest choices first.
- When you come to a difficult word, use it in a sentence. Repeat the sentence, substituting your answer choices. The answer that fits best in the sentence is probably the correct one.
- Some matching items contain phrases rather than single words. Begin with the column that has the most words. This column will usually give the most information.
- Work down one column at a time. It is confusing to switch back and forth.

Testing It Out

Now look at the sample questions more closely.

Think: The first column is a list of art projects, and the second column lists tools that can be used to make these art projects.

A *photograph* is made with a *camera*, so I see that the answer is choice **B**.

I think that a *mural* is a type of painting. *Paintbrushes* are used to paint things, and I see that choice **D** is *paintbrush*, so the answer to number 2 is **D**.

A *collage* is something that you make out of scraps. I don't see that listed under the second column, but choice **A** is *scissors*. You can use *scissors* to make scraps. So logically, **A** is the correct answer.

The last word in the first column is *cartoon*. The only remaining choice in the second column is *pencil*, which is definitely something that you can use to make a *cartoon*. So the answer to number 4 is **C**.

Matching Practice

Directions: For numbers 1–8, match words or phrases that go together.

1 George Washington	A 1861	**1** Ⓐ Ⓑ Ⓒ Ⓓ
2 Abraham Lincoln	B 1801	**2** Ⓐ Ⓑ Ⓒ Ⓓ
3 Thomas Jefferson	C 1901	**3** Ⓐ Ⓑ Ⓒ Ⓓ
4 Theodore Roosevelt	D 1789	**4** Ⓐ Ⓑ Ⓒ Ⓓ

5 millimeter	F 1000 meters	**5** Ⓕ Ⓖ Ⓗ Ⓙ
6 centimeter	G 0.001 meter	**6** Ⓕ Ⓖ Ⓗ Ⓙ
7 decimeter	H 0.01 meter	**7** Ⓕ Ⓖ Ⓗ Ⓙ
8 kilometer	J 0.1 meter	**8** Ⓕ Ⓖ Ⓗ Ⓙ

Directions: For numbers 9–16, match the words with opposite meanings.

9 ostracize	A foggy	**9** Ⓐ Ⓑ Ⓒ Ⓓ
10 lucid	B regular	**10** Ⓐ Ⓑ Ⓒ Ⓓ
11 despicable	C welcome	**11** Ⓐ Ⓑ Ⓒ Ⓓ
12 sporadic	D laudable	**12** Ⓐ Ⓑ Ⓒ Ⓓ

13 ravenous	F friendly	**13** Ⓕ Ⓖ Ⓗ Ⓙ
14 discordant	G persuade	**14** Ⓕ Ⓖ Ⓗ Ⓙ
15 sinister	H full	**15** Ⓕ Ⓖ Ⓗ Ⓙ
16 dissuade	J harmonious	**16** Ⓕ Ⓖ Ⓗ Ⓙ

Analogy Questions

In an analogy question, you must figure out the relationship between two things. Then you must complete another pair with the same relationship.

EXAMPLE | **Rain is to downpour as snow is to _____.**

        (A) blinding   (C) flurry

        (B) blizzard   (D) monsoon

Analogies usually have two pairs of items. In the question above, the two pairs are *rain/downpour* and *snow/_____*. To answer analogy questions, do the following:

• Find the missing item that completes the second pair. To do this, figure out how the first pair of items relate to each other. Form a sentence that explains how they are related.

• Next, use your sentence to figure out the missing word in the second pair of items.

• For more difficult analogies, try each answer choice in the sentence you formed. Choose the answer that fits best.

• Think about whether you are looking for a noun, verb, adjective, or other part of speech as you look for your answer.

Testing It Out

Now look at the sample question more closely.

Think: I'll make a sentence out of the first pair: "When there is a *downpour*, there is a lot of *rain*." The new sentence I need to complete is "When there is a _____, there is a lot of snow."

I've heard people talk about *blinding* snowstorms before, but choice **A** doesn't fit into my sentence. "When there is a *blinding*, there is a lot of *snow*." That doesn't make any sense.

If I insert choice **B** into my sentence, I get "When there is a *blizzard*, there is a lot of snow." That's definitely true. I'll note **B** as a good choice.

Choice **C** would be "When there is a *flurry*, there is a lot of snow." That's not true—a snow *flurry* means that there won't be a lot of snow. That choice is wrong.

D would be "When there is a *monsoon*, there is a lot of *snow*." People use the word *monsoon* when they are talking about the jungle. Rain falls in jungles, not snow. So **D** is not the correct answer.

I'll choose **B**, *blizzard*, as my answer.

Analogy Practice

Directions: Find the word that best completes each analogy.
Fill in the circle next to your answer.

1 <u>Yen</u> is to <u>Japan</u> as dollar is to _____.

Ⓐ dime
Ⓑ Washington, D.C.
Ⓒ United States
Ⓓ nickel

2 <u>Fish</u> is to <u>trout</u> as <u>mammal</u> is to _____.

Ⓕ dolphin   Ⓗ goldfish
Ⓖ halibut   Ⓙ iguana

3 <u>Apartment</u> is to <u>mansion</u> as <u>bicycle</u> is to _____.

Ⓐ tricycle   Ⓒ fancy
Ⓑ minivan   Ⓓ sports car

4 <u>Scrutinize</u> is to <u>skim</u> as <u>strip</u> is to _____.

Ⓕ furniture   Ⓗ bare
Ⓖ mar   Ⓙ embellish

5 <u>Dogma</u> is to <u>belief</u> as <u>freedom</u> is to _____.

Ⓐ disbelief   Ⓒ libation
Ⓑ arrest   Ⓓ liberty

6 <u>Lion</u> is to <u>pride</u> as <u>goose</u> is to _____.

Ⓕ herd   Ⓗ gaggle
Ⓖ hubris   Ⓙ snob

7 <u>Grapes</u> are to <u>raisins</u> as <u>plum</u> is to _____.

Ⓐ apples   Ⓒ sweet
Ⓑ prune   Ⓓ plume

8 <u>Animal</u> is to <u>biologist</u> as <u>weather</u> is to _____.

Ⓕ meteorologist   Ⓗ scientist
Ⓖ archeologist   Ⓙ newscaster

9 <u>et cetera</u> is to <u>etc.</u> as <u>World Wide Web</u> is to _____.

Ⓐ internet   Ⓒ WWF
Ⓑ WWW   Ⓓ HTML

10 <u>City</u> is to <u>hamlet</u> as <u>ocean</u> is to _____.

Ⓕ pond   Ⓗ rain
Ⓖ water   Ⓙ beach

Short Answer Questions

Some test questions don't give you answers to choose from. Instead, you must write short answers in your own words. These are called "short answer" or "open response" questions.

EXAMPLE

It was Maria's worst nightmare. Her family was leaving Chicago, where she was born and raised, and moving to the countryside. She loved the excitement of the city, and she would miss her friends.

When she arrived at her new house, she was surprised at how beautiful the country was. She was amazed at how far she could see. In Chicago, tall buildings prevented great views. Down the street from her new home, she saw other kids playing softball. Maybe her new home wouldn't be so bad after all.

1 **What is the main idea of this passage?** _____

2 **Do you think Maria will be happy in her new home? How do you know?**

_____

When you write short answers to questions, do the following:

• Read each question carefully. Make sure to respond directly to the question that is being asked, not to details or statements that are given elsewhere in the body of the question.

• Your response should be short but complete. Don't waste time including unnecessary information in your answer, but be sure to answer the entire question, not just part of it.

• Write in complete sentences unless the directions say you don't have to.

• Make sure to double-check your answers for spelling, punctuation, and grammar.

Testing It Out

Now look at the sample questions more closely.

Think: Even though she loves Chicago, Maria will learn to love her new home. So I will write:

1. *The main idea of this story is that even if you have to leave a place that you love, you can learn to love a new place.*

2. *I think that Maria will definitely be happy in her new home. The countryside is beautiful. Even though it is different than Chicago, Maria will learn to love it. Although Maria had to leave her friends, she will make new ones.*

Short Answer Practice

Directions: Read the passage below. Then answer the questions.

Leadbelly's Legacy

When you play your favorite rock or rap CD, you probably don't realize that you are enjoying the legacy of "Leadbelly." Born in 1888, Huddie Ledbetter, nicknamed "Leadbelly," was a blues guitarist who inspired generations of musicians.

For much of Huddie Ledbetter's life, he wandered from place to place, playing anywhere he could. In 1934 he was discovered by John and Alan Lomax, who helped him find a larger audience for his music. Soon he was playing in colleges, clubs, and music halls. He was featured on radio and television shows.

Leadbelly died in 1949, but his music lives on. Musicians in every style credit him with laying the foundation for today's popular music. From rock and roll to rap, American music owes a great debt to Leadbelly.

What is the author's purpose for writing this passage? How do you know?

_____

_____

_____

What is the topic sentence of this passage?

_____

_____

What was the turning point of Leadbelly's career? Why?

_____

_____

In your own words, tell why musicians today talk about Leadbelly.

_____

_____

Reading

Many standardized tests have sections called "Reading" or "Reading Comprehension." Reading Comprehension questions test your ability to read for details, find meaning in a sentence or passage, and use context clues to figure out words or ideas you don't understand. The following is a list of topics covered on Reading Comprehension tests. Look at the tips and examples that go with each topic.

Word Meaning

Word meaning questions test your vocabulary and your ability to figure out unfamiliar words. Keep these tips in mind when answering questions about word meaning:

- Use **prefixes** and **suffixes** to help you understand a word's meaning.
- Use the surrounding words to help you guess the meaning of a new word.

Literal and Inferential Comprehension

You will be asked to read short passages and think about their meanings in two ways. In **literal comprehension** questions, you will be asked about specific details from the story. You can find the answers by going back to the passage and reading carefully. You will also be asked about the sequence of events—this means you will need to know the order in which events happened in the story.

In **inferential comprehension** questions, you will be required to draw conclusions or make predictions based on what you've read. These questions can be harder to answer. If you are not sure about your answers, start by eliminating unreasonable choices.

Main Idea

You will be asked to identify the main idea of some of the passages you read. The **main idea** should tell what the story is all about.

Style and Genre

You will probably be asked to identify the **genre**, or category of literature, to which a passage belongs. Genre categories include science fiction, fantasy, adventure, persuasive writing, and newspaper articles.

- You may also be asked to describe the techniques the writer uses in the passage. These may include:

  simile a comparison using *like* or *as*
  metaphor a comparison of two different objects
  personification a description that gives an object lifelike qualities

Reading Practice

Directions: For numbers 1–3, choose the word that means the same as the underlined word.

1 **a <u>pompous</u> attitude**

   Ⓐ delightful   Ⓑ optimistic   Ⓒ haughty   Ⓓ negative

2 **a brilliant <u>scheme</u>**

   Ⓕ color   Ⓖ plan   Ⓗ comment   Ⓙ act

3 **a <u>grueling</u> task**

   Ⓐ upsetting   Ⓑ exciting   Ⓒ demanding   Ⓓ unfair

Directions: For numbers 4 and 5, read the passage and then answer the questions.

Kenya's Confidence

When Kenya discovered the stone on the beach, its beauty dazzled her. It was the color of the evening sea and the texture of marble. It was just the perfect size to fit in her palm. When Kenya rubbed her stone, she felt stronger. The stone gave her confidence, and she kept it in her pocket all the time. When she had to do something that was formerly difficult for her, such as talking in class, she would rub the stone.

For two years, Kenya had dreamed of getting a part in the school musical. The drama teacher, Mr. Hughes, didn't know Kenya, and she had always been too shy to go to the auditions and introduce herself. This year, with the help of her stone, Kenya felt inspired to try out. At the audition she sat, rubbing the stone nervously in her pocket, until her name was called. She had been practicing all week, and knew the words perfectly. As her audition began, her voice rang out across the stage. She was no longer Kenya but the character from the musical. When she finished her song, she heard vigorous applause. She looked up to see Mr. Hughes smiling. "Well, Kenya," he said. "You are a talented performer."

Kenya couldn't believe it. Walking off the stage, she reached in her pocket to give the stone a squeeze of thanks. Her fingers found nothing but emptiness. The stone was gone.

4 **In this passage, the word "formerly" means**

   Ⓕ in the future.   Ⓗ in the past.

   Ⓖ annoyingly.   Ⓙ joyfully.

5 **How did Mr. Hughes feel about Kenya's performance?**

   Ⓐ disturbed   Ⓒ impressed

   Ⓑ amused   Ⓓ disappointed

Language Arts

Language Mechanics and Expression

Standardized tests usually include sections that contain questions about spelling, grammar, punctuation, capitalization, and sentence structure. These sections are often called "Language Mechanics and Expression" or "Language Arts."

The following is a list of topics included under Language Mechanics and Expression. Look at the tips and examples that go with each topic. If you have trouble with one of the topics listed, talk to your teacher or parent for extra help.

Grammar

Grammar is the set of rules that helps you write clear sentences. When you answer a multiple choice question, write a short answer, or respond to a writing prompt, remember:

- how to use different parts of speech such as **nouns**, **verbs**, **adjectives**, **prepositions**, **adverbs**, and **pronouns**
- an adjective describes a noun, and an adverb describes a verb. **Articles** (*a, an, the*) are short words that point out specific nouns.

> The | brown | mouse | darted | swiftly
> *article   adjective   noun   verb   adverb*
> | into | the | hole.
> *preposition article   noun*

- A **direct object** is a noun that receives the action of a verb.

> The pitcher threw <u>the ball</u>.

- An indirect object is a noun that names the person for whom something is done.

> Can you throw <u>me</u> the ball?

Capitalization and Punctuation

You will be asked questions about capitals and punctuation marks. You will also be required to use them when you write answers in your own words. Remember:

- All sentences start with a capital letter.
- Capitalize all proper nouns and proper adjectives.

> <u>M</u>y brother and <u>I</u> saw a bear at <u>G</u>lacier <u>N</u>ational <u>P</u>ark in <u>M</u>ontana.

 **Remember**

Start each sentence with a capital letter.

Capitalize all proper nouns and proper adjectives.

Language Arts

- All sentences should end with a period (.), a question mark (?), or an exclamation point (!). Pick the one that best fits the meaning of the sentence.
- Use quotation marks around the words that a character says.

> "Look up in the sky!" I yelled.
> "What is it?" my brother asked.
> "It looks like a bald eagle," I replied.

- Use apostrophes effectively to show possession or contraction.

> Let's go! We can't be late.
> We've already packed Mom's car.

Spelling

You may be asked to find words spelled correctly or words that are spelled incorrectly. You should also check your own spelling when you write.

(incorrect) Their were many activitys to joyn at the comunity center.

(correct) There were many activities to join at the community center.

Sentence Structure

Use complete sentences whenever you write a short answer or paragraph on a test. You may also be asked questions about individual sentences. Keep in mind the parts of a complete sentence:

- The **subject** is the part of the sentence that is doing something.

> The star of the show waved to her cheering audience.

- The **predicate** is the part of the sentence that tells what the subject is doing.

> The star of the show waved to her cheering audience.

Also keep in mind:

- A **topic sentence** introduces the main idea at the beginning of a paragraph.
- A **concluding sentence** ends the paragraph by summarizing the most important information.

Remember

Check your spelling as you write.

Language Arts Practice

Directions: For numbers 1 and 2, look at the underlined part of the sentence. Choose the answer that shows the best capitalization and punctuation for that part. Mark the space for "Correct as it is" if the underlined part is correct.

1 Sherry went to <u>soccer practice. and then</u> she went home.

    Ⓐ practice, and
    Ⓑ practice; and
    Ⓒ practice. And
    Ⓓ Correct as it is

2 Mr. <u>Jones, my teacher,</u> showed us how make birdhouses.

    Ⓕ Jones my teacher,
    Ⓖ Jones; my teacher
    Ⓗ Jones my teacher
    Ⓙ Correct as it is

Directions: For numbers 3 and 4, choose the word that is spelled correctly and best completes the sentence.

3 We sent Mary a card to _____ her.

    Ⓐ congradulate
    Ⓑ congratulate
    Ⓒ congratulatte
    Ⓓ congradulayt

4 This book has an _____ plot.

    Ⓕ unbelevable
    Ⓖ unbeliveable
    Ⓗ unbileveable
    Ⓙ unbelievable

Directions: For numbers 5 and 6, choose the correct answer to each question.

5 What is the simple predicate of this sentence?

Jim and Tyrone interviewed their parents for a class project.

    Ⓐ Jim
    Ⓑ Tyrone
    Ⓒ interviewed
    Ⓓ for

6 What is the direct object of this sentence?

The referee tossed the team captain the ball.

    Ⓕ team
    Ⓖ referee
    Ⓗ ball
    Ⓙ captain

Language Arts Practice

Directions: For numbers 7 and 8, choose the sentence that is complete and correctly written.

7 Ⓐ Suddenly, us heard a loud crash form upstairs.

Ⓑ I told her to give me the book after she had finished it.

Ⓒ He can't sing too good, but his music is very popular.

Ⓓ Her and I went to the library to study for our exams.

8 Ⓕ Afterward Aisha and Sue went for an ice cream.

Ⓖ Because of the threat of tornadoes, plane was not able to take off.

Ⓗ Careful records of the day's work in the file folders.

Ⓙ Writing the paper for her class, Jeanie felt confident that she would do well.

Directions: For questions 9 and 10, read the paragraphs and choose the best topic sentence for each paragraph.

9 **Most sea otters live near the North Pacific Ocean. They have hind feet shaped like flippers that allow them to swim easily on their backs. Sea otters even float on their backs while they eat, sleep, and carry their babies. They can also stay underwater longer than most other mammals—almost four minutes!**

Ⓐ The sea otter is a fascinating mammal.

Ⓑ This helps them hunt for food such as clams, crabs, fish, and squid.

Ⓒ Mammals are interesting creatures.

Ⓓ Sea otters are adorable.

10 **The black box keeps track of information during a flight. It records how fast the plane is flying and how high it is above the ground. It also records information about the equipment and the actions of the pilots. When a plane crashes, investigators use it to find out what went wrong.**

Ⓕ Flying in an airplane is the best way to travel to distant destinations.

Ⓖ Black boxes are not necessarily black.

Ⓗ Pilots use complicated navigation equipment when flying a plane.

Ⓙ Airplanes usually carry a device called a flight data recorder, or a *black box.*

Writing

Many tests will ask you to respond to a writing prompt. A writing prompt is a question or statement that you are asked to respond to.

> **EXAMPLE** **Think about a new way of doing something in school. Explain why your idea is a good one. Give reasons that will persuade your school to use your idea.**

The following is a list of guidelines to use when responding to a writing prompt.

Read the Prompt
- Read the instructions carefully. Sometimes you will be given a choice of questions or topics to write about. You don't want to respond to more questions than you need to.
- Once you have located the prompt to answer, read it twice to be sure you understand it. Remember, there is no one right response to a writing prompt. There are only stronger and weaker arguments.

Prewrite
- Before you write your answer, jot down some details to include.
- You may find it helpful to use a chart, web, illustration, or outline to help you organize the information you want to include in your response.
- Even if you aren't asked to, it is always a good idea to include facts and examples to support your answer. If the prompt asks you to respond to a reading passage, include specific examples from the passage to strengthen your argument.

Draft
- Begin your answer with a **topic sentence** that answers the main question and gives the main idea.
- Write **supporting sentences** that give details and tell more about your main idea. All of these sentences should relate to the topic sentence.

Proofread
- Make sure to proofread your draft for missing words, grammar, punctuation, capitalization, indentation, and spelling. Correct your mistakes.

Writing Practice

Directions: Write a three- or four-paragraph response to **one** of the questions below.

- **Do you think all students should be required to take standardized tests at the end of each school year? Provide at least three reasons that support your argument.**

- **Imagine that you could be a superhero. Write a description of what you would look like, what your superpower would be, and how you would use it.**

_____

_____

_____

_____

_____

_____

_____

_____

_____

_____

_____

_____

_____

_____

_____

_____

_____

_____

Math: Draw a Diagram

Math Problems

Many standardized tests will ask you to solve math story problems. Sometimes these are also called word problems. You have probably already done problems like this in school, so this format will not be new to you. When you see story problems on a test, though, you will have limited time to find your answer.

Use the following strategies to help solve story problems quickly. Remember that not every strategy can be used with every story problem. You will have to choose the best strategy to use for each one.

Draw a Diagram

Sometimes you can draw a diagram to help solve a math problem. Diagrams can help you to see the action of a problem and find a correct solution. Diagrams can often help you solve geometry problems.

> **EXAMPLE** **Rocco's band is having an outdoor concert, so Rocco built a stage that is 24 feet long and 38 feet wide. What is the perimeter of the stage?**
>
> Ⓐ 62 feet Ⓑ 124 feet Ⓒ 912 feet Ⓓ 1246 feet

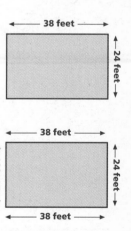

- Draw your diagram of a rectangle and label the information you are given in the problem. Use the information you are given to determine any other information you need to solve the problem.
- The formula for perimeter is *length* + *length* + *width* + *width*, so you need to find the measurements of all four sides of the rectangle.
- Since you know that parallel sides of a rectangle are the same length you can determine the length and width of every side of the rectangle.
- You can then add the sides together, 24 feet + 24 feet + 38 feet + 38 feet = 124 feet. **B** is the correct answer.

When you draw a diagram:
- ☐ Read the problem carefully.
- ☐ Determine what data you need to solve the problem.
- ☐ Base your diagram on the data in the problem.
- ☐ Find how you can use the data in your diagram to solve the problem.
- ☐ Solve the problem.

Diagram Practice

Directions: For numbers 1–4, draw a diagram to help solve each problem.

1 **An irregularly shaped pentagon has a perimeter of 764 meters. The pentagon has sides that are 129 meters, 365 meters, 24 meters, and 100 meters long. What is the length of the fifth side?**

   Ⓐ   146 meters

   Ⓑ   177 meters

   Ⓒ 1,389 meters

   Ⓓ   22 meters

2 **You know the measurements of 2 angles in a triangle. They are 72 degrees and 42 degrees. What is the measurement of the third angle?**

   Ⓕ   66 degrees

   Ⓖ   27 degrees

   Ⓗ 114 degrees

   Ⓙ   14 degrees

3 **A round table has a diameter of 6 feet. What is the circumference of the table?**

   Ⓐ 18.00 feet

   Ⓑ   6.34 feet

   Ⓒ 12.00 feet

   Ⓓ 18.84 feet

   $$C = \pi \times d$$
   $$\pi \approx 3.14$$

4 **David's swimming pool is 42 feet long, 16 feet wide, and 8 feet deep. What is the volume of David's swimming pool?**

   $$length \times width \times height = volume$$

   Ⓕ   66 cubic feet

   Ⓖ 5,376 cubic feet

   Ⓗ 15,376 cubic feet

   Ⓙ 28,502 cubic feet

Math: Trick Questions

Some test questions contain the word *not*. You must be careful to notice when the word *not* is used. These are a type of trick question; you are being tested to see if you have read and understood the material completely.

EXAMPLE **Which number is not equivalent to the mixed number $6\frac{4}{5}$?**

    Ⓐ 6.8

    Ⓑ $\frac{102}{15}$

    Ⓒ $\frac{34}{5}$

    Ⓓ 3.4

When solving this type of problem, first figure out how the word *not* applies to it. In this case you must find the number that is not equivalent to $6\frac{4}{5}$. Check the possible answers to see which one is not equivalent to $6\frac{4}{5}$.

- 6.8 is the decimal equivalent of $6\frac{4}{5}$.
- $\frac{102}{15}$ is an equivalent fraction.
- $\frac{34}{5}$ is $6\frac{4}{5}$ written as a fraction.
- 3.4 is *not* equivalent to $6\frac{4}{5}$.

The correct answer **D**, since the other choices are all equivalent to $6\frac{4}{5}$.

When you have the word *not* in a problem:
- ❑ Read the problem carefully.
- ❑ Determine what information you need to solve the problem.
- ❑ Compare all of the possible answer choices.
- ❑ Solve the problem.

Remember

Watch out for trick questions, especially those that have the word *not* in them.

Trick Questions Practice

Directions: For numbers 1–6, choose the correct answer. Remember to look carefully for the word *not*.

1 The Screaming Decibels posted fliers for their first concert. They made 145 copies of the flier at 3 cents a copy. How much did it cost to make the fliers?

Ⓐ $43.50

Ⓑ $14.50

Ⓒ $4.35

Ⓓ $1.45

2 There are 1,267 students in Fort Lee. On Friday night, 233 students go to a concert, 589 go to a carnival, and 60 go to the movies. How many students total are not going to a concert?

Ⓕ 1,034 students

Ⓖ 385 students

Ⓗ 882 students

Ⓙ 233 students

3 Of the 87,725 residents of Page County, 37,968 are registered voters. How many residents are not registered voters?

Ⓐ 125,693

Ⓑ 37,968

Ⓒ 49,757

Ⓓ None of the above

4 The Art Appreciation Club wants to hold a series of exhibits. They have saved $3000 to host them. It costs $1495 to book a large exhibit hall and $575 to book a small one. If they book two small halls and one large hall, how much money will they have left?

Ⓕ $355.50

Ⓖ $355.00

Ⓗ $155.00

Ⓙ None of the above

5 The Morris School Band needs $575 to go on a trip. If they hold a car wash and charge $7 per car, how many cars must they wash to raise enough money?

Ⓐ 81 cars

Ⓑ 82 cars

Ⓒ 83 cars

Ⓓ 79 cars

6 At the zoo there are a total of 685 animals. There are 423 mammals and 136 birds. How many animals are not mammals or birds?

Ⓕ 559   Ⓗ 126

Ⓖ 262   Ⓙ 549

Math: Paper and Pencil

On tests it often helps to work a problem out using paper and pencil. This helps you to visualize the problem and double-check your answer. It is especially useful when you must solve an equation.

> **EXAMPLE** At 7:22 P.M. Sherlock Holmes sets out after evil mastermind, Professor Moriarty. It takes Moriarty 20 minutes to get to the train station. Always one step ahead, it takes Sherlock $\frac{4}{5}$ of the time to get to the station. At what time does Sherlock arrive at the station to apprehend Moriarty?
>
> _____

Here you are not given any answers to choose from; you must figure out the answer using a paper and pencil.

Use paper and pencil to multiply 20 by $\frac{4}{5}$. This will give you the total number of minutes it took Sherlock to get to the train station.

$$20 \times \frac{4}{5} = \frac{80}{5} = 16 \text{ minutes}$$

Then use paper and pencil to find out when Sherlock Holmes arrived at the train station to apprehend Professor Moriarty.

$$7:22 \text{ P.M.} + 16 = 7:38 \text{ P.M.}$$

Now use paper and pencil again to check the answer you found the first time. You know the answer is 7:38 P.M.

When you use pencil and paper:
- ☑ Read the problem carefully.
- ☑ Write neatly so that you do not make errors.
- ☑ Solve the problem.
- ☐ Check your work.

Paper and Pencil Practice

Directions: Find the answers to numbers 1–5. Use the work area to show your work.

1 Miles and Nina go to the mall. Nina has $\frac{3}{4}$ as much money as Miles. If Miles has $28, how much money does Nina have?

1

2 Robert wants to buy a Hawaiian shirt. The shirt was originally $32, but now it is 20% less. How much does the shirt now cost?

2

3 Felice goes to the arcade to play skeeball. One target is worth 100 points. A second target is worth 10 points. The point value of a third target is $\frac{1}{2}$ of the difference between 100 and 10. How much is the third target worth?

3

4 Jim has won 6 tickets playing skeeball and 32 tickets playing Fling the Frog. Temporary tattoos cost 8 tickets each. How many temporary tattoos can Jim get?

4

5 Sela wants to buy two sodas. She only has nickels. If each soda costs 60 cents, how many nickels does she need to buy two sodas?

5

Math: Guess and Check

One way to solve a word problem is to make your best guess and then work backwards to check your answer.

EXAMPLE   **17 more than 5 times *y* is 142. What is *y*?**

Ⓐ 20

Ⓑ 29

Ⓒ 22

Ⓓ 25

First, try choosing a reasonable answer choice from the choices you have been given. Imagine that your guess for this answer is **C**, 22.

$$22 \times 5 = 110$$
$$110 + 17 = 127$$
$$\text{Check: } 127 < 142$$

Since your number was too small, you know you should try a larger number. Guess **D**, 25.

$$25 \times 5 = 125$$
$$125 + 17 = 142$$
$$\text{Check: } 142 = 142$$

Your guess is correct. $25 \times 5 + 17 = 142$. The correct answer is **D**.

When you use the guess and check method:

❏ Read the problem carefully.

❏ Make a reasonable first guess.

❏ Revise your guess based on whether your answer was too high or low.

❏ Check that your answer is reasonable based on the question.

 **Remember**

Sometimes it's OK to guess. Then work backwards to make sure your guess is reasonable.

Guess and Check Practice

Directions: For numbers 1–6, use the guess-and-check method to help you solve the problems.

1 Two numbers have a product of 216 and quotient of 6. What are the two numbers?

  Ⓐ 116 and 4

  Ⓑ 36 and 6

  Ⓒ 152 and 2

  Ⓓ 80 and 5

2 Ellen is playing her favorite game. In this game, vowels are worth 2 points, and most consonants are worth 1 point. The letters Q and W are both worth 5 points. Ellen has a word that is worth 16 points. What word has she spelled?

  Ⓕ whenever

  Ⓖ question

  Ⓗ whether

  Ⓙ None of the above

3 Bob the entomologist has collected some ants, spiders, and centipedes. Ants have 6 legs, spiders have 8 legs, and centipedes have 100 legs. How many of each insect is there if there are 448 legs in all?

  Ⓐ 32 ants, 7 spiders, 2 centipedes

  Ⓑ 62 ants, 14 spiders, 1 centipede

  Ⓒ 31 ants, 8 spiders, 2 centipedes

  Ⓓ 34 ants, 6 spiders, 2 centipedes

4 Two numbers have a product of 18,259 and a difference of 558. What are the two numbers?

  Ⓕ 589 and 31

  Ⓖ 662 and 106

  Ⓗ 576 and 20

  Ⓙ 823 and 264

5 Two numbers have a sum of $8\frac{5}{12}$ and a product of $1\frac{3}{8}$. What are the two numbers?

  Ⓐ $\frac{2}{3}$ and $7\frac{1}{6}$

  Ⓑ $7\frac{3}{8}$ and $\frac{2}{3}$

  Ⓒ $\frac{1}{6}$ and $8\frac{1}{4}$

  Ⓓ $8\frac{1}{8}$ and $\frac{1}{12}$

6 5 more than 4 times x is 113. What is x?

  Ⓕ 25

  Ⓖ 23

  Ⓗ 28

  Ⓙ 27

Math: Estimation

Use estimation to help you narrow down answer choices on a multiple choice test.

EXAMPLE **Mattie is shipwrecked on a desert island. She chronicles her adventures each day in a journal that she rescued from her beached ship. Mattie writes about 562 words a day. If she has written 53,952 words in all, how many days has she been shipwrecked?**

   Ⓐ 101 days

   Ⓑ   96 days

   Ⓒ   94 days

   Ⓓ   87 days

First, estimate the answer by rounding up or down. Round to the most precise place needed for the problem. In this case, to the nearest ten.

> 562 rounds to 560
> 53,952 rounds to 53,950
> 53,950 ÷ 560= 96.339

You can cross off choices **A** and **D** since they are far out of your estimated range. Then find the exact answer by dividing:

$$562\overline{)53{,}952}^{96}$$

So **B** is the correct answer.

When you estimate an answer:
- ☐ Read the problem carefully.
- ☐ Round the numbers you need to estimate the answer.
- ☐ Estimate the answer.
- ☐ Eliminate any answers not close to your estimate.
- ☐ Find the exact answer.

Estimation Practice

Directions: For numbers 1–6, use estimation to solve the problems.

1 There are 36 buccaneers, 52 pirates, and 116 shipmates sailing the seven seas. One ship holds 22 people. How many ships are sailing the seven seas?

Ⓐ 6 ships

Ⓑ 9 ships

Ⓒ 10 ships

Ⓓ 13 ships

2 Rita, Lulu, and Molly dig up a treasure chest that contains $3876 worth of gold and jewels. If they split the loot evenly, how much money will each girl have?

Ⓕ $1292

Ⓖ $952

Ⓗ $1506

Ⓙ $1330

3 Gilbert cooks chili for his friends. For each pot of chili, Gilbert needs 14 ounces of tomatoes. If Gilbert has 86 ounces of tomatoes, how many pots of chili can he make?

Ⓐ 3

Ⓑ 7

Ⓒ 4

Ⓓ 6

4 A triangular shaped ship's sail is 54.6 meters tall and 28.4 meters wide at its base. What is the area of the sail?

Ⓕ 689.5 meters

Ⓖ 752.7 meters

Ⓗ 862.6 meters

Ⓙ 775.3 meters

5 On a canoe trip with his family, Pete travels an average of 27 miles a day. If the final destination is 140 miles away, about how long will it take Pete to get there?

Ⓐ 2 days

Ⓑ 7 days

Ⓒ 5 days

Ⓓ 12 days

6 A person needs about 2.5 quarts of water each day to survive. For how many days could a person survive on 40 quarts of water?

Ⓕ 100 days

Ⓖ 16 days

Ⓗ 20 days

Ⓙ 14 days

Math: Incomplete Information

Some test problems may include "not enough information" as one of the answer choices. When you see a problem with this as an answer choice, watch out! The problem may not contain enough information for you to solve it.

 What is the area of the triangle?

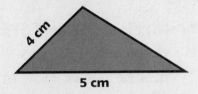

4 cm

5 cm

Ⓐ   9 square centimeters
Ⓑ   10 square centimeters
Ⓒ   12 square centimeters
Ⓓ   Not enough information

Determine what information is given in the problem and the picture.

—The triangle has one side that is 4 cm long.

—The triangle has a base that is 5 cm wide.

—To find the area of a triangle you have to multiply $\frac{1}{2}$ base $\times$ the height.

Since you do not know the height of the triangle, you do not have enough information to answer the question. Reread the problem to verify that you do not have enough information to solve it.

Since you do not have enough information, **D** is your answer.

 When you think you don't have enough information to solve a problem:
☐ Read the problem carefully.
☐ Determine what information you need to solve the problem.
☐ Check to see if you have all the information to solve the problem.
☐ Verify that the information you need to solve the problem is missing.

Incomplete Information Practice

Directions: For numbers 1–6, choose the correct answer to each problem.

1 Jamal is a football player. In one play, he ran the ball from the 63rd yard line to the 74th yard line. Then he ran the ball to the 92nd yard line. How far did Jamal run in all?

Ⓐ 29 yards
Ⓑ 32 yards
Ⓒ 35 yards
Ⓓ Not enough information

2 Tamara is competing in a karate tournament. Tamara spars with 14 people. To win a sparring match, Tamara must score 5 points. How many points has Tamara scored?

Ⓕ 60 points
Ⓖ 65 points
Ⓗ 70 points
Ⓙ Not enough information

3 Katie decided to buy 4 comic books. Each book cost the same amount of money, and Katie received $2.04 in change. How much money did each comic book cost?

Ⓐ $2.50
Ⓑ $3.95
Ⓒ $4.50
Ⓓ Not enough information

4 Nikolai has saved $18.73 for a skateboard. He has $\frac{1}{5}$ of the money that he needs. How much does the skateboard cost?

Ⓕ $93.65
Ⓖ $94.75
Ⓗ $102.50
Ⓙ Not enough information

5 Kiki is running in a ten mile race. If she runs at her usual rate, how long will it take her to finish the race?

Ⓐ 1 hour and 15 minutes
Ⓑ 1 hour and 20 minutes
Ⓒ 1 hour and 30 minutes
Ⓓ Not enough information

6 The perimeter of a rectangular room is 90 feet. If the length of the room is 35 feet, how wide is the room?

Ⓕ 8 feet
Ⓖ 10 feet
Ⓗ 20 feet
Ⓙ Not enough information

Math: Use a Calculator

You may be allowed to use a calculator with some standardized tests. Using a calculator can save you time, especially when you need to compute multi-digit numbers. A calculator can also allow you to double-check your work quickly.

EXAMPLE $6^8 =$

  Ⓐ   48
  Ⓑ   216
  Ⓒ   46,656
  Ⓓ   1,679,616

To solve the problem, you must write the multiplication sentence in which 6 is shown 8 times.

$$6 \times 6 \times 6 \times 6 \times 6 \times 6 \times 6 \times 6 = ?$$

Then key the sentence into your calculator to find the answer. Be sure to key in the correct numbers to find the correct answer! The correct answer is **D**.

When you use a calculator:
- ☐ Read the problem carefully.
- ☐ Be sure you key in the correct numbers.
- ☐ Solve the problem.
- ☐ Check to see that your answer is reasonable.

Calculator Practice

Directions: For numbers 1–8, choose the correct answer.

1 The volcano Kilauea is $2^{12} - 87$ feet tall. How tall is Kilauea?

  Ⓐ   28 feet
  Ⓑ   960 feet
  Ⓒ 4,096 feet
  Ⓓ 4,009 feet

2 Yuri Gagarin became the first man in space in the year $9^3 + 8^3 + 3^6 - 9$. When did Yuri go to space?

  Ⓕ 1954
  Ⓖ 1961
  Ⓗ 1968
  Ⓙ 1977

3 The Amazon River is $4(852 + 148)$ miles long. How long is the Amazon River?

  Ⓐ 4,000 miles
  Ⓑ 4,500 miles
  Ⓒ 4,700 miles
  Ⓓ 5,200 miles

4 56^3 divided by 4 =

  Ⓕ   18
  Ⓖ   168
  Ⓗ 43,904
  Ⓙ 116,716

5 $5^4 + 125$ students go to South High School. How many students go to South?

  Ⓐ 1,225 students
  Ⓑ   750 students
  Ⓒ   625 students
  Ⓓ   550 students

6 $78,125 \div (16 + 9) =$

  Ⓕ 1,275
  Ⓖ 3,125
  Ⓗ 2,560
  Ⓙ   60

7 $5(72.08 \times .04) =$

  Ⓐ 360.6
  Ⓑ 144.16
  Ⓒ 360.4
  Ⓓ   14.416

8 Texas is $8^6 + 5,133$ square miles. What is the area of Texas?

  Ⓕ   37,901 square miles
  Ⓖ 262,144 square miles
  Ⓗ 267,277 square miles
  Ⓙ   5,181 square miles

Math: Computation

Most standardized tests contain math sections where you must solve a variety of number equations. These questions test your ability to find exact answers to math problems. You will often be allowed to use scrap paper to work out these problems, but the work you show on scrap paper will not count.

Using Operations

Your ability to perform basic mathematical operations (such as addition, subtraction, multiplication, and division) will be tested. Whenever you are solving a math equation, be sure of which operation you must use to solve the problem.

The following are operations you may be tested on and how you will be expected to use them:

- multiply two- and three-digit numbers and greater
- divide two- and three-digit numbers and greater
- divide by one- and two-digit numbers
- multiply integers, fractions, decimals
- divide whole numbers, fractions, decimals
- multiply with percentages
- multiply and divide by powers of 10
- add and subtract fractions and mixed numbers

Even though you will be given answer choices, it's best to work the problem out first using scrap paper. Then you can compare the answer you found to the choices that are given. If you have time, double-check your answer to each problem by using the inverse operation.

Other Things to Keep in Mind

If you ever solve computation problems involving decimals, make sure your answer choice shows the decimal point in the correct place.

If your problem contains units, be sure that you find the answer choice with the correct units labeled. Many tests will try to confuse you by substituting one unit for another in an answer choice.

Finally, if you get to a tough problem, look carefully at the answer choices and use logic to decide which one makes the most sense. Then plug this choice into the equation and see if it works.

Remember

It's always a good idea to work the problem out first using scrap paper.

Computation Practice

Directions: For numbers 1–8, find the correct answer to each problem.

1 74.864 – 43.925 =

   (A) 30.903
   (B) 30.939
   (C)   3.939
   (D)   3.093

2 3,918 ÷ 6 =

   (F) 653
   (G) 650.3
   (H) 605
   (J) 523

3 $937.25 + $31.56 + $87.34 =

   (A) $937.54
   (B) $968.81
   (C) $1056.15
   (D) $1276.98

4 $\frac{3}{4} + \frac{1}{20} + \frac{1}{2} =$

   (F) $\frac{7}{4}$
   (G) $1\frac{3}{10}$
   (H) $\frac{3}{10}$
   (J) $\frac{6}{2}$

5 337 × .16 =

   (A) 539.2
   (B) 542
   (C) 54.21
   (D) 53.92

6 **Which of the following fractions is equal to 83.33%?**

   (F) $\frac{5}{6}$
   (G) $\frac{1}{8}$
   (H) $\frac{2}{5}$
   (J) Not enough information

7 498 × 6.55 =

   (A) 32619
   (B) 3261.9
   (C) 326.19
   (D) 32.619

8 $689.25 – $53.69 + $9.99 =

   (F) $645.55
   (G) $752.93
   (H) $635.56
   (J) $625.57

Math: Concepts

Standardized tests also test your understanding of important math concepts you will have learned about in school.

Number Concepts

You may have to show that you understand the following number concepts:

- recognizing the standard and metric units of measure used for weighing and finding length and distance
- reading a thermometer
- recognizing prime numbers
- finding multiples, factors, and averages
- writing and reading expanded notation
- calculating to powers of ten
- finding square roots
- reading and writing roman numerals

Geometry

It's also common to see questions about geometry on standardized tests. You may be asked to:

- recognize parallel and perpendicular lines, rays, and segments
- identify solid shapes such as prisms, spheres, cubes, cylinders, and cones
- find the area and perimeter of flat shapes
- find the area, perimeter, and volume of solid shapes
- find the line of symmetry in a flat shape
- recognize right, obtuse, and acute angles
- find the radius, diameter, and circumference of a circle
- recognize polygons

Other Things to Keep in Mind

The best way to prepare for concept questions is to study math words and definitions in advance. However, if you come to a difficult problem, think of what you do know about the topic and eliminate answer choices that don't make sense. For example, if you are asked to identify a shape that you don't recognize, you may recognize some of other shapes mentioned and know that they couldn't be correct. Use the process of elimination whenever you come to a tough question.

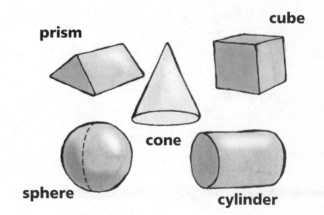

 **Remember**

Study math words and definitions in advance.

Eliminate answer choices that don't make sense.

Concepts Practice

Directions: For numbers 1–6, choose the correct answer to each problem.

1 **What are all of the factors of 36?**

Ⓐ 2, 3, 6, 12

Ⓑ 1, 2, 3, 4, 6, 8, 12, 24, 36

Ⓒ 1, 2, 3, 4, 12, 36

Ⓓ 1, 2, 3, 4, 6, 9, 12, 18, 36

2 **A circle has a diameter of 5 cm. What is the circumference of the circle?**

Ⓕ 15.7 centimeters

Ⓖ 16 centimeters

Ⓗ 15.5 centimeters

Ⓙ 16.7 centimeters

3 **81 cubed =**

Ⓐ 9

Ⓑ 243

Ⓒ 5,314

Ⓓ None of the above

4 **Which one of these number sentences is false?**

Ⓕ $\frac{1}{2} > \frac{1}{4}$

Ⓖ 0.006 > 0.06

Ⓗ $\frac{1}{8} = 0.125$

Ⓙ 8.7 > 8.07

5 **What is the volume of a fish tank with a length of 3 meters, a height of 2 meters, and a width of 2 meters?**

Ⓐ 7 cubic feet

Ⓑ 9 cubic feet

Ⓒ 12 cubic feet

Ⓓ None of the above

6 **Which of the following is an obtuse angle?**

Ⓕ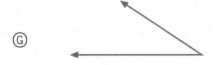

Ⓖ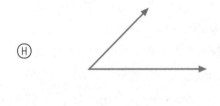

Ⓗ

Ⓙ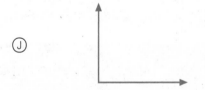

Math: Applications

You will often be asked to apply what you know about math to a new type of problem or set of information. Even if you aren't exactly sure how to solve a problem of this type, you can usually draw on what you already know to make the most logical choice.

When preparing for standardized tests, you may want to practice:

- how to use a number line with whole numbers and decimals
- recognizing complex number patterns and object patterns and extending them
- reading bar graphs, tally charts, or pictographs
- reading pie charts and line and double-line graphs
- reading and making Venn diagrams
- plotting x-y coordinates
- finding ratios, probability, least common multiples, prime and common factors
- using the order of operations

Other Things to Keep in Mind

When answering application questions, be sure to read each problem carefully. You may want to use scrap paper to work out some problems.

Again, if you come to a problem you aren't sure how to solve or a word/idea you don't recognize, try to eliminate answer choices by using what you do know. Then go back and check your answer choice in the context of the problem.

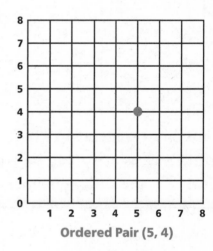

Ordered Pair (5, 4)

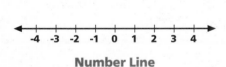

Number Line

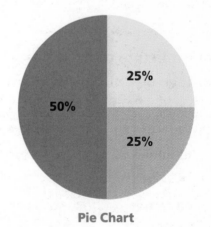

Pie Chart

Applications Practice

Directions: For numbers 1–5, choose the correct answer to each problem.

1 **What is the next number in this pattern?**

3, 9, 27, 81, ____

Ⓐ 84 Ⓒ 243

Ⓑ 90 Ⓓ None of the above

2 **What are the coordinates of point F?**

Ⓕ (6, 5)

Ⓖ (5, 6)

Ⓗ (4, 3)

Ⓙ (3, 4)

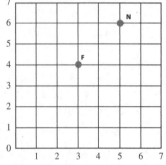

3 **If 8 out of 20 students in Mrs. Winslow's class are going on a field trip, what is the ratio of students who are going to students who are not going?**

Ⓐ 2 : 3 Ⓒ 4 : 5

Ⓑ 5 : 2 Ⓓ 5 : 4

4 **If you wanted to compare the percentage of students who are going on the field trip, to the percentage of students who are not going on the field trip, what would be the best graphic to use?**

Ⓕ a line graph Ⓗ a pie chart

Ⓖ a Venn diagram Ⓙ Not enough information

5 **This line graph shows how many people visit the Smallville Museum of Art each year.**

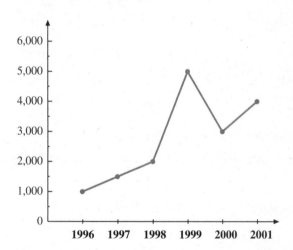

Which of the following statements is true?

Ⓐ The Smallville Museum of Art had $\frac{1}{3}$ as many visitors in 1996 than in 2000.

Ⓑ The Smallville Museum of Art had 50% more visitors in 2001 than in 1998.

Ⓒ The Smallville Museum of Art has seen a steady increase in visitors since 1996.

Ⓓ The Smallville Museum of Art had twice as many visitors in 1997 than in 1996.

Social Studies

Standardized tests often include questions about social studies topics. You may see questions about maps, geography, history, and government.

The following is a list of topics that may be covered on the test and tips to use when solving the questions. Sample questions are also included.

Map Skills

You will probably be asked to look at a map and answer questions about it. Keep these tips in mind:

- A map can include a **compass rose**, a **legend** with symbols, and a scale.
- Lines of latitude (horizontal) and longitude (vertical) are the grid lines on maps that help to describe the location of specific places.
- Different maps serve different purposes, such as political maps, physical maps, relief maps, population maps, and topographical maps.

When you read a map, be sure to read the title first so that you understand the kind of information that is being presented.

Geography

Geography is the study of the land and its features. You should know these terms:

- **natural features:** plateau, bay, peninsula, island, isthmus, coastline, butte, cape, delta, strait, mesa, archipelago, savanna, tributary
- **other geography terms:** hemisphere, equator, prime meridian, continent

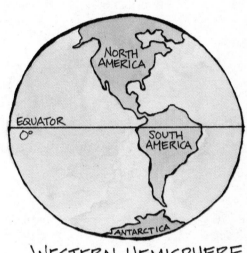

WESTERN HEMISPHERE

Compass Rose

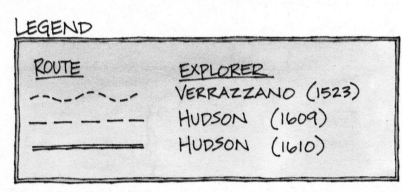

Social Studies

Time Lines

A **time line** organizes historical events in chronological order. Some questions will ask you to use a time line to answer a question:

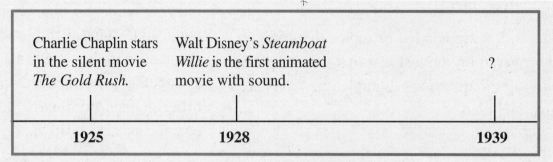

EXAMPLE

Charlie Chaplin stars in the silent movie *The Gold Rush.*

Walt Disney's *Steamboat Willie* is the first animated movie with sound.

?

1925   1928   1939

Which event most likely took place in 1939?

Ⓐ Walt Disney builds a theme park in Paris.
Ⓑ Charlie Chaplin stars in an animated movie.
Ⓒ *The Wizard of Oz* uses new color film technologies.
Ⓓ *Steamboat Willie* comes out on DVD.

The correct answer is **C**. Even if you are not sure of the correct answer, it is easy to eliminate the unreasonable choices, **A**, **B**, and **D**.

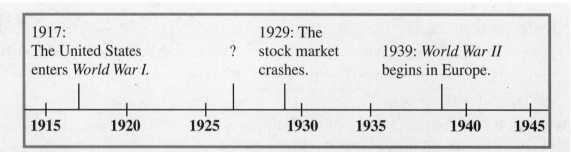

EXAMPLE

1917: The United States enters *World War I.*

?

1929: The stock market crashes.

1939: *World War II* begins in Europe.

1915   1920   1925   1930   1935   1940   1945

Which event most likely took place in 1927?

Ⓕ Texas joins the Union.
Ⓖ The Civil War ends.
Ⓗ Lewis and Clark explore the Louisiana Territory.
Ⓙ Charles Lindbergh flies across the Atlantic Ocean.

The correct answer is **J**. Even if you are not sure, you can eliminate the unreasonable choices, **F**, **G**, and **H**.

Social Studies

Reading Passages

You will probably be asked to read a passage about a social studies topic and to answer questions about it. Keep these tips in mind:

- Before you read, look at the questions first so that you know what kind of information you are looking for.
- Look for key words: *who*, *what*, *when*, *where*, and *why*. These will help you focus on the relevant information in the passage.
- As you read, keep in mind the purpose of the passage: what does the writer want you to learn?
- Look for cause and effect relationships. When you read about an event, look for the reasons that tell why it happened and what happened as a result.

Research Skills

Some questions will test your ability to think like a historian. You will be asked about different sources that historians use to find historical data. You may need to know:

- different factual sources for doing historical research, like books, encyclopedias, and newspaper articles
- parts of books that help you do research effectively, like a table of contents or an index

Social Studies Knowledge

Some social studies questions will ask specific questions about topics you have been studying in class.

You may be asked questions about the rise and expansion of important civilizations such as:

- the Roman Empire
- Islamic civilizations
- Chinese and Japanese civilizations
- West African civilizations
- Medieval Europe

You may be asked questions about certain times and movements, such as:

- the Renaissance
- the Reformation
- the Scientific Revolution

As you answer these questions, make sure you understand what the question is asking. Get rid of the unreasonable answers first, and then make your best guess.

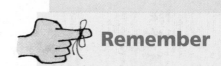 **Remember**

Before you read a passage, look at the questions first so that you will know what kind of information you are looking for.

Social Studies Practice

Directions: For numbers 1 and 2, study the map and answer the questions that follow.

Directions: For numbers 3–5, choose the correct answer.

1 **On what continent would you find Egypt?**

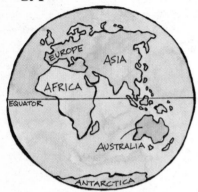

Ⓐ Asia

Ⓑ Africa

Ⓒ Europe

Ⓓ South America

2 **Most of the fertile land in Ancient Egypt is located in**

Ⓕ Lower Egypt.

Ⓖ Libyan Desert.

Ⓗ Thebes.

Ⓙ Upper Egypt.

3 **Ancient Egypt was ruled by**

Ⓐ a parliament.

Ⓑ a pharaoh.

Ⓒ a president.

Ⓓ an emperor.

4 **During which period was there a period of cultural rebirth in Europe?**

Ⓕ the Middle Ages

Ⓖ the Renaissance

Ⓗ the Dark Ages

Ⓙ the Roman Empire

5

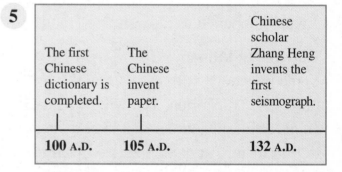

The first Chinese dictionary is completed.	The Chinese invent paper.	Chinese scholar Zhang Heng invents the first seismograph.
100 A.D.	105 A.D.	132 A.D.

What would be a good title for this time line?

Ⓐ Dynasties of Ancient China

Ⓑ Technical Achievements in Modern China

Ⓒ Construction of the Great Wall of China

Ⓓ Technical Achievements in Ancient China

Social Studies Practice

Directions: For numbers 6–8, read the passage and answer the questions that follow.

Black Death

In the 14th century, a plague called the Black Death swept through Europe, killing approximately one-fourth of the population. No one knew how to explain the disease. Some said that the Black Death descended upon Europe because of an unusual alignment of the planets. Others thought that humanity was being punished for its immorality.

Medieval physicians suggested many theories, but no one suspected that the Black Death was being passed to humans by the rats and fleas that thrived in filthy and unsanitary cities.

Because medieval doctors did not understand why and how the disease was being spread, they did not know how to treat it. Some physicians thought you could ward off the disease by wearing a small bouquet of flowers around your neck, or by sitting by a fireplace. Others prescribed prayer or bloodletting with leeches. Those who had money fled the overcrowded cities, in the hopes that they could avoid the plague by staying in the countryside.

6 **Medieval physicians were unable to stop the plague because _____**

- Ⓕ they hadn't developed the drugs to treat plague victims.
- Ⓖ they were dead.
- Ⓗ they didn't know what caused the plague.
- Ⓙ they wore small bouquets of flowers around their neck.

7 **The author's purpose is _____**

- Ⓐ to tell you a funny story about medieval physicians.
- Ⓑ to give you information about the way the plague spread and was treated.
- Ⓒ to give you information about the way modern doctors treat the plague.
- Ⓓ to persuade you to move to the country in the hopes of avoiding the plague.

8 **The best place to look for more information on the plague is _____**

- Ⓕ a book called *Rats!*
- Ⓖ an internet page about bouquet arranging.
- Ⓗ a pamphlet on medieval bloodletting.
- Ⓙ an encyclopedia entry on the 14th century.

Science

You will often see science questions on standardized tests. These questions may be about scientific facts. They may also test your ability to "think like a scientist." This means you must use data (information) to make predictions and draw conclusions. The following list of tips includes some words you will need to know. It also contains examples of the types of science questions you may see on a test.

Science Vocabulary

Many science questions will include at least one of the words below:

- **research question** the question that a scientist asks
- **hypothesis** a scientist's possible answer to the question
- **experiment** a test to see if the hypothesis is correct
- **prediction** a guess about the future results of an experiment
- **observation** when a scientist watches the results of an experiment
- **data** the information collected in an experiment
- **conclusion** a statement based on information gathered in an experiment
- **dependent variable** an element of the experiment that changes with each different trial
- **controlled variable** an element of the experiment that stays the same while other elements change

Science Processes

Some science questions will ask you to answer questions about the scientific process. Keep in mind the steps of a scientific experiment and use your common sense as you examine your choices.

EXAMPLE **A scientist wants to find out how diet affects the growth of different breeds of dogs. Which variable should she change in each of her trials in order to answer her question?**

    Ⓐ the type of food   Ⓒ the dogs

    Ⓑ the setting   Ⓓ the amount of food

The correct answer is **C** because she is testing the effect of a certain type of food on different breeds of dogs. Therefore, each trial should be repeated with a different breed of dog while the temperature remains constant.

Science

Reading Graphs

Standardized tests will often include graphs showing the results of an experiment. You may be asked to read the graph or to use the data to predict or draw a conclusion.

Science Knowledge

Science questions on your standardized test may require you to know specific scientific information. This may include information about:

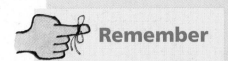

Remember

Use common sense.

Eliminate unreasonable answers first.

- forces and motion
- interpreting information from an experiment or report
- Earth's systems (natural disasters, erosion and weathering, natural resources) and its movement in space
- atoms
- physical and chemical properties of substances
- ecosystems (relationships between producers, consumers, and decomposers)
- cell biology (plant cells vs. animal cells)
- internal systems of the human body (respiratory, digestive)
- comparing and contrasting traits that enhance survival

If you don't know the answer to a specific question, use your common sense. An excellent strategy is to eliminate unreasonable answers first.

EXAMPLE **Which of the following is a physical change?**

   Ⓐ rusting metal
   Ⓑ burning wood
   Ⓒ dissolving salt
   Ⓓ rotting apple

In this example, you can easily eliminate **A**, **B**, and **D** because you know that these changes can not be reversed and therefore a chemical change has occurred. The correct answer is **C**, because when you dissolve salt into water, the salt can still be retrieved unchanged. A chemical change has not occurred.

Science Practice

Directions: Find the correct answer to numbers 1–6.

1 **Which of the following is a function of the circulatory system?**

(A) breaking food into fuel

(B) passing oxygen into the bloodstream

(C) moving blood throughout the body

(D) cleaning blood and sending waste to the bladder

2 **What does a decomposer do?**

(F) makes its own food using light or chemical energy

(G) ingests other living organisms in a food chain

(H) provides a habitat for other organisms

(J) breaks down plant and animal matter into nutrients

3 **The walls of plant cells are composed mainly of**

(A) cellulose.

(B) membranes.

(C) vacuoles.

(D) chloroplasts.

4 **What causes the moon to appear to change shape?**

(F) changes in the amount of sunlight reflected by Earth

(G) the sun's rotation around the moon and Earth

(H) change in the amount of light the moon produces

(J) changes in the amount of sunlight reflected by the moon toward Earth

5 **What is the freezing point of water in degrees Fahrenheit?**

(A) 0°F

(B) 100°F

(C) 32°F

(D) 212°F

6 **The smallest unit of an element which still has all the properties of that element is called**

(F) a gram.

(G) a cell.

(H) an atom.

(J) a compound.

Introduction
Practice Test and Final Test

The remainder of this book is made up of two tests. On page 79, you will find a Practice Test. On page 125, you will find a Final Test. These tests will give you a chance to put the tips you have learned to work. There is also a name and answer sheet preceding each test and an answer key at the end of the book.

Here are some things to remember as you take these tests:

• Be sure you understand all the directions before you begin each test.

• Ask an adult questions about the directions if you do not understand them.

• Work as quickly as you can during each test. There are no time limits on the Practice Test, but you should try to make good use of your time. There are suggested time limits on the Final Test to give you practice managing your time.

• You will notice little GO and STOP signs at the bottom of the test pages. When you see a GO sign, continue on to the next page if you feel ready. The STOP sign means you are at the end of a section. When you see a STOP sign, take a break.

• Work as quickly as you can during each test. There are not time limits, but you should make good use of your time.

• When you change an answer, be sure to erase your first mark completely.

• You can guess at an answer or skip difficult items and go back to them later.

• Use the tips you have learned whenever you can.

• After you have completed your tests, check your answers with the answer key. You can record the number of questions you got correct for each unit on the recording sheet on page 76.

• It is OK to be a little nervous. You may even do better.

• When you complete all the lessons in this book, you will be on your way to test success!

Table of Contents

Practice Test

Answer Sheet 77

Unit 1 Reading
Lesson 1: Reading Nonfiction 79
Lesson 2: Reading Fiction 88
Lesson 3: Review 91

Unit 2 Language Arts
Lesson 1: Vocabulary 94
Lesson 2: Language Mechanics 96
Lesson 3: Spelling 98
Lesson 4: Writing 99
Lesson 5: Review 101

Unit 3 Mathematics
Lesson 1: Computation 105
Lesson 2: Mathematics Skills 106
Lesson 3: Review 111

Unit 4 Social Studies
Lesson 1: Social Studies 115
Lesson 2: Review 117

Unit 5 Science
Lesson 1: Science 119
Lesson 2: Review 121

Final Test

Answer Sheet 123

Unit 1
Reading 125

Unit 2
Language Arts 131
   Writing 138

Unit 3
Mathematics 140

Unit 4
Social Studies 149

Unit 5
Science 151

Name Sheet

This is a practice name sheet like the ones you will use in school. Follow these directions:

1. Use a No. 2 pencil.
2. Write your name in the boxes. Put only one letter in each box. Then fill in one little circle below each letter that matches that letter of your name.
3. Fill in all the other information.

On the back of this page is your Answer Sheet. Fill in only one letter for each item. If you change an answer, make sure to erase your first mark completely.

STUDENT'S NAME

LAST | FIRST | MI

SCHOOL

TEACHER

FEMALE ◯   MALE ◯

BIRTHDATE

MONTH	DAY	YEAR

JAN, FEB, MAR, APR, MAY, JUN, JUL, AUG, SEP, OCT, NOV, DEC

(Bubble grid with letters A–Z for name columns, and numbered circles 0–9 for birthdate Day and Year.)

GRADE
(4) (5) (6) (7) (8)

Name and Answer Sheet

Record Your Scores

After you have completed and checked each test, record your scores below. Do not count your answers for the sample questions or the writing pages.

Practice Test

Unit 1 Reading
Number of Questions: 38   Number Correct _____

Unit 2 Language Arts
Number of Questions: 47   Number Correct _____

Unit 3 Mathematics
Number of Questions: 33   Number Correct _____

Unit 4 Social Studies
Number of Questions: 22   Number Correct _____

Unit 5 Science
Number of Questions: 20   Number Correct _____

Final Test

Unit 1 Reading
Number of Questions: 31   Number Correct _____

Unit 2 Language Arts
Number of Questions: 49   Number Correct _____

Unit 3 Mathematics
Number of Questions: 41   Number Correct _____

Unit 4 Social Studies
Number of Questions: 9   Number Correct _____

Unit 5 Science
Number of Questions: 10   Number Correct _____

Practice Test Answer Sheet

Fill in only one letter for each item. If you change an answer, make sure to erase your first mark completely.

Unit 1: Reading, pages 79–93

A Ⓐ Ⓑ Ⓒ Ⓓ	**8** Ⓕ Ⓖ Ⓗ Ⓙ	**17** Ⓐ Ⓑ Ⓒ Ⓓ	**25** Ⓕ Ⓖ Ⓗ Ⓙ	**33** Ⓕ Ⓖ Ⓗ Ⓙ
B Ⓕ Ⓖ Ⓗ Ⓙ	**9** Ⓐ Ⓑ Ⓒ Ⓓ	**18** Ⓕ Ⓖ Ⓗ Ⓙ	**26** Ⓐ Ⓑ Ⓒ Ⓓ	**34** Ⓐ Ⓑ Ⓒ Ⓓ
1 Ⓐ Ⓑ Ⓒ Ⓓ	**10** Ⓕ Ⓖ Ⓗ Ⓙ	**19** Ⓐ Ⓑ Ⓒ Ⓓ	**27** Ⓕ Ⓖ Ⓗ Ⓙ	**35** Ⓕ Ⓖ Ⓗ Ⓙ
2 Ⓕ Ⓖ Ⓗ Ⓙ	**11** Ⓐ Ⓑ Ⓒ Ⓓ	**20** Ⓕ Ⓖ Ⓗ Ⓙ	**28** Ⓐ Ⓑ Ⓒ Ⓓ	**36** Ⓐ Ⓑ Ⓒ Ⓓ
3 Ⓐ Ⓑ Ⓒ Ⓓ	**12** Ⓕ Ⓖ Ⓗ Ⓙ	**21** Ⓐ Ⓑ Ⓒ Ⓓ	**29** Ⓕ Ⓖ Ⓗ Ⓙ	**37** Ⓕ Ⓖ Ⓗ Ⓙ
4 Ⓕ Ⓖ Ⓗ Ⓙ	**13** Ⓐ Ⓑ Ⓒ Ⓓ	**22** Ⓕ Ⓖ Ⓗ Ⓙ	**30** Ⓐ Ⓑ Ⓒ Ⓓ	**38** Ⓐ Ⓑ Ⓒ Ⓓ
5 Ⓐ Ⓑ Ⓒ Ⓓ	**14** Ⓕ Ⓖ Ⓗ Ⓙ	**23** Ⓐ Ⓑ Ⓒ Ⓓ	**31** Ⓕ Ⓖ Ⓗ Ⓙ	
6 Ⓕ Ⓖ Ⓗ Ⓙ	**15** Ⓐ Ⓑ Ⓒ Ⓓ	**C** Ⓐ Ⓑ Ⓒ Ⓓ	**D** Ⓐ Ⓑ Ⓒ Ⓓ	
7 Ⓐ Ⓑ Ⓒ Ⓓ	**16** Ⓕ Ⓖ Ⓗ Ⓙ	**24** Ⓐ Ⓑ Ⓒ Ⓓ	**32** Ⓐ Ⓑ Ⓒ Ⓓ	

Unit 2: Language Arts, pages 94–103

A Ⓐ Ⓑ Ⓒ Ⓓ	**10** Ⓕ Ⓖ Ⓗ Ⓙ	**20** Ⓕ Ⓖ Ⓗ Ⓙ	**29** Ⓕ Ⓖ Ⓗ Ⓙ	**40** Ⓐ Ⓑ Ⓒ Ⓓ
1 Ⓐ Ⓑ Ⓒ Ⓓ	**11** Ⓐ Ⓑ Ⓒ Ⓓ	**21** Ⓐ Ⓑ Ⓒ Ⓓ	**30** Ⓐ Ⓑ Ⓒ Ⓓ	**41** Ⓕ Ⓖ Ⓗ Ⓙ
2 Ⓕ Ⓖ Ⓗ Ⓙ	**12** Ⓕ Ⓖ Ⓗ Ⓙ	**22** Ⓕ Ⓖ Ⓗ Ⓙ	**31** Ⓕ Ⓖ Ⓗ Ⓙ	**42** Ⓐ Ⓑ Ⓒ Ⓓ
B Ⓕ Ⓖ Ⓗ Ⓙ	**C** Ⓐ Ⓑ Ⓒ Ⓓ	**D** Ⓐ Ⓑ Ⓒ Ⓓ Ⓔ	**32** Ⓐ Ⓑ Ⓒ Ⓓ	**43** Ⓕ Ⓖ Ⓗ Ⓙ
3 Ⓐ Ⓑ Ⓒ Ⓓ	**13** Ⓐ Ⓑ Ⓒ Ⓓ	**23** Ⓐ Ⓑ Ⓒ Ⓓ	**33** Ⓕ Ⓖ Ⓗ Ⓙ	**F** Ⓐ Ⓑ Ⓒ Ⓓ Ⓔ
4 Ⓕ Ⓖ Ⓗ Ⓙ	**14** Ⓕ Ⓖ Ⓗ Ⓙ	**24** Ⓕ Ⓖ Ⓗ Ⓙ	**34** Ⓐ Ⓑ Ⓒ Ⓓ	**44** Ⓐ Ⓑ Ⓒ Ⓓ Ⓔ
5 Ⓐ Ⓑ Ⓒ Ⓓ	**15** Ⓐ Ⓑ Ⓒ Ⓓ	**25** Ⓐ Ⓑ Ⓒ Ⓓ	**35** Ⓕ Ⓖ Ⓗ Ⓙ	**45** Ⓕ Ⓖ Ⓗ Ⓙ Ⓚ
6 Ⓕ Ⓖ Ⓗ Ⓙ	**16** Ⓕ Ⓖ Ⓗ Ⓙ	**26** Ⓕ Ⓖ Ⓗ Ⓙ Ⓚ	**36** Ⓐ Ⓑ Ⓒ Ⓓ	**46** Ⓐ Ⓑ Ⓒ Ⓓ Ⓔ
7 Ⓐ Ⓑ Ⓒ Ⓓ	**17** Ⓐ Ⓑ Ⓒ Ⓓ	**27** Ⓐ Ⓑ Ⓒ Ⓓ Ⓔ	**37** Ⓕ Ⓖ Ⓗ Ⓙ	**47** Ⓕ Ⓖ Ⓗ Ⓙ Ⓚ
8 Ⓕ Ⓖ Ⓗ Ⓙ	**18** Ⓕ Ⓖ Ⓗ Ⓙ	**E** Ⓐ Ⓑ Ⓒ Ⓓ	**38** Ⓐ Ⓑ Ⓒ Ⓓ	
9 Ⓐ Ⓑ Ⓒ Ⓓ	**19** Ⓐ Ⓑ Ⓒ Ⓓ	**28** Ⓐ Ⓑ Ⓒ Ⓓ	**39** Ⓕ Ⓖ Ⓗ Ⓙ	

Practice Test Answer Sheet

Unit 3: Mathematics, pages 105–114

A Ⓐ Ⓑ Ⓒ Ⓓ Ⓔ	**7** Ⓐ Ⓑ Ⓒ Ⓓ	**16** Ⓕ Ⓖ Ⓗ Ⓙ	**23** Ⓐ Ⓑ Ⓒ Ⓓ Ⓔ	**31** Ⓐ Ⓑ Ⓒ Ⓓ
B Ⓕ Ⓖ Ⓗ Ⓙ Ⓚ	**8** Ⓕ Ⓖ Ⓗ Ⓙ	**17** Ⓐ Ⓑ Ⓒ Ⓓ	**24** Ⓕ Ⓖ Ⓗ Ⓙ Ⓚ	**32** Ⓕ Ⓖ Ⓗ Ⓙ
1 Ⓐ Ⓑ Ⓒ Ⓓ Ⓔ	**9** Ⓐ Ⓑ Ⓒ Ⓓ	**18** Ⓕ Ⓖ Ⓗ Ⓙ	**F** Ⓐ Ⓑ Ⓒ Ⓓ	**33** Ⓐ Ⓑ Ⓒ Ⓓ
2 Ⓕ Ⓖ Ⓗ Ⓙ Ⓚ	**10** Ⓕ Ⓖ Ⓗ Ⓙ	**D** Ⓐ Ⓑ Ⓒ Ⓓ Ⓔ	**25** Ⓐ Ⓑ Ⓒ Ⓓ	
3 Ⓐ Ⓑ Ⓒ Ⓓ Ⓔ	**11** Ⓐ Ⓑ Ⓒ Ⓓ	**E** Ⓕ Ⓖ Ⓗ Ⓙ Ⓚ	**26** Ⓕ Ⓖ Ⓗ Ⓙ	
4 Ⓕ Ⓖ Ⓗ Ⓙ Ⓚ	**12** Ⓕ Ⓖ Ⓗ Ⓙ	**19** Ⓐ Ⓑ Ⓒ Ⓓ Ⓔ	**27** Ⓐ Ⓑ Ⓒ Ⓓ Ⓔ	
C Ⓐ Ⓑ Ⓒ Ⓓ	**13** Ⓐ Ⓑ Ⓒ Ⓓ	**20** Ⓕ Ⓖ Ⓗ Ⓙ Ⓚ	**28** Ⓕ Ⓖ Ⓗ Ⓙ Ⓚ	
5 Ⓐ Ⓑ Ⓒ Ⓓ	**14** Ⓕ Ⓖ Ⓗ Ⓙ	**21** Ⓐ Ⓑ Ⓒ Ⓓ Ⓔ	**29** Ⓐ Ⓑ Ⓒ Ⓓ Ⓔ	
6 Ⓕ Ⓖ Ⓗ Ⓙ	**15** Ⓐ Ⓑ Ⓒ Ⓓ	**22** Ⓕ Ⓖ Ⓗ Ⓙ Ⓚ	**30** Ⓕ Ⓖ Ⓗ Ⓙ Ⓚ	

Unit 4: Social Studies, pages 115–118

1 Ⓐ Ⓑ Ⓒ Ⓓ	**6** Ⓕ Ⓖ Ⓗ Ⓙ	**11** Ⓐ Ⓑ Ⓒ Ⓓ	**16** Ⓕ Ⓖ Ⓗ Ⓙ	**21** Ⓐ Ⓑ Ⓒ Ⓓ
2 Ⓕ Ⓖ Ⓗ Ⓙ	**7** Ⓐ Ⓑ Ⓒ Ⓓ	**12** Ⓕ Ⓖ Ⓗ Ⓙ	**17** Ⓐ Ⓑ Ⓒ Ⓓ	**22** Ⓕ Ⓖ Ⓗ Ⓙ
3 Ⓐ Ⓑ Ⓒ Ⓓ	**8** Ⓕ Ⓖ Ⓗ Ⓙ	**13** Ⓐ Ⓑ Ⓒ Ⓓ	**18** Ⓕ Ⓖ Ⓗ Ⓙ	
4 Ⓕ Ⓖ Ⓗ Ⓙ	**9** Ⓐ Ⓑ Ⓒ Ⓓ	**14** Ⓕ Ⓖ Ⓗ Ⓙ	**19** Ⓐ Ⓑ Ⓒ Ⓓ	
5 Ⓐ Ⓑ Ⓒ Ⓓ	**10** Ⓕ Ⓖ Ⓗ Ⓙ	**15** Ⓐ Ⓑ Ⓒ Ⓓ	**20** Ⓕ Ⓖ Ⓗ Ⓙ	

Unit 5: Science, pages 119–122

1 Ⓐ Ⓑ Ⓒ Ⓓ	**5** Ⓐ Ⓑ Ⓒ Ⓓ	**9** Ⓐ Ⓑ Ⓒ Ⓓ	**13** Ⓐ Ⓑ Ⓒ Ⓓ	**17** Ⓐ Ⓑ Ⓒ Ⓓ
2 Ⓕ Ⓖ Ⓗ Ⓙ	**6** Ⓕ Ⓖ Ⓗ Ⓙ	**10** Ⓕ Ⓖ Ⓗ Ⓙ	**14** Ⓕ Ⓖ Ⓗ Ⓙ	**18** Ⓕ Ⓖ Ⓗ Ⓙ
3 Ⓐ Ⓑ Ⓒ Ⓓ	**7** Ⓐ Ⓑ Ⓒ Ⓓ	**11** Ⓐ Ⓑ Ⓒ Ⓓ	**15** Ⓐ Ⓑ Ⓒ Ⓓ	**19** Ⓐ Ⓑ Ⓒ Ⓓ
4 Ⓕ Ⓖ Ⓗ Ⓙ	**8** Ⓕ Ⓖ Ⓗ Ⓙ	**12** Ⓕ Ⓖ Ⓗ Ⓙ	**16** Ⓕ Ⓖ Ⓗ Ⓙ	**20** Ⓕ Ⓖ Ⓗ Ⓙ

Lesson 1 | Reading Nonfiction

SAMPLE A

When Lawrence looked closely at the old barn, he found that the posts and beams were in good shape. The roof was also solid, so there was a good chance the barn could be saved.

Lawrence is probably planning to

A move the barn.

B raise horses.

C tear the barn down.

D rebuild the barn.

Directions: Choose the best topic sentence for the paragraph.

SAMPLE B

_____. **Squirrels make their homes with leaves and twigs high in a tree. Beavers make lodges out of sticks and mud.**

F Animals do unusual things.

G People aren't the only animals that build homes.

H Weather influences what animals do.

J Natural materials can be used in many ways.

Before you begin to answer questions, look at each page in the section on which you are working.

Skim the story, then skim the questions.

Answer the easiest questions first.

BUILDING OUR WORLD

From our earliest history, human beings have built everything from small huts to huge monuments. On the following pages, you will learn more about an architect and the materials we use to build.

GO

Directions: Here is the story of a woman who became an important architect. Although many people know about the buildings she designed, very few people know about the architect herself. Read the story, then do numbers 1–10.

MARY COLTER

In 1958, one of America's most important architects died. Even though most people don't know her name, the mark she left on American architecture will always be with us.

Mary Elizabeth Jane Colter was born in Pennsylvania in 1869. She was raised in Minnesota, and from an early age Colter was interested in art, specifically the art of Native Americans. When she was in her twenties, her family moved to San Francisco, giving Mary a chance to pursue her interests in art and design. She worked in an architecture office as an apprentice and attended the California School of Design. She studied with a number of talented architects who greatly influenced her.

At the turn of the century, Colter returned to St. Paul, Minnesota, to teach at the Mechanic Arts High School. She became involved in her community and lectured frequently on architecture. Mary was soon prominent in artistic circles. In 1902, she was called to Albuquerque to design a downtown showroom for Native American artwork and jewelry. This project was very satisfying for Mary, and it marked the beginning of her loyal attachment to the Southwest.

Her next assignments were at the Grand Canyon in northern Arizona. Colter spent considerable time there, learning about Native American art and gaining an appreciation for the landscape. Over the next few decades, she designed several structures in and around the Grand Canyon, including cabins and rest stops for hikers and trail riders. All were constructed using local materials and fit well into their

GO

80

natural setting. The most famous of these is the Desert View Watchtower.

This 70-foot stone tower, inspired by ancient Native American designs, stands at the east entrance to the Grand Canyon and provides visitors with a panoramic view of the canyon. The stone and steel tower was completed in 1933, and its irregular surface and varied shades of stone match the look and colors of the canyon itself. The interior of the structure was decorated with Native American art by another artist, so a visit to this tower is a trip into local history.

In between her Grand Canyon projects, Mary created several more modern structures along a noted railroad line. The most famous of these is La Posada in Winslow, Arizona. Completed in 1930, it is Colter's architectural masterpiece. Lying alongside the Santa Fe Railroad and historic Route 66, this huge Colonial ranch hotel and railway station was a challenge for the architect. She was not satisfied with just designing the building; she insisted on creating every part of the inn, down to its doorknobs. Once again, she was able to use her artistic abilities to make a structure part of its historical and geographic settings.

Although she never became famous, Mary Colter worked steadily her whole life. When she wasn't designing inns, she was working on restaurants, shops, or even dining cars on trains. She set many artistic standards with her work, and her style has been imitated by many other architects. Perhaps her greatest tribute is that five of her buildings have been named National Historic Landmarks.

GO

1 **Mary showed that she was serious about art by**

A designing buildings at a very early age.

B making her hobby drawing and painting.

C becoming a famous Native American artist.

D going to an art school and becoming an apprentice.

2 **The story you just read is mostly about**

F how to become an architect.

G a woman who became an architect.

H a woman who became very famous.

J how to build inns and restaurants.

3 **Exploring the answers to which of these questions would lead to a better understanding of Colter's job as an architect?**

A Why did she go to school in San Francisco?

B What were her favorite kinds of buildings?

C What did she do during her work day?

D How do buildings become historic landmarks?

4 **Which of the following best states the main idea of this story?**

F Most of the famous architects we have heard of are men.

G Mary Colter did important things but is not well known.

H Architecture is less important now that Mary Colter is gone.

J Women like Mary Colter had very few career choices.

5 **Which of these best describes Mary Colter?**

A gifted

B impatient

C old-fashioned

D distracted

6 **The answer you chose for number 5 is best because you learned from the story that**

F Mary changed her mind often.

G Mary had a lot of artistic skills.

H Mary was difficult to work with.

J Mary resisted modern ideas.

GO

7 **Choose the sentence that best combines these sentences into one.**

Mary Colter was an important architect.

Colter was important because she set new standards.

Colter was important because she met many artistic challenges.

A Being important as an architect, Mary Colter was important in setting new standards and meeting many artistic challenges.

B Mary Colter was an important architect because she set new standards and met many artistic challenges.

C Setting new standards, Mary Colter was an important architect because she met many artistic challenges.

D She was an important architect because Mary Colter set new standards and met many artistic challenges.

8 **Choose the sentence that is complete and written correctly.**

F Considered to be one of the best architects.

G Designing buildings the thing she liked.

H Mary inspired by Native American art.

J Mary moved to California with her family.

9 **Appreciating Native American art probably helped Mary Colter in her career by**

A giving her knowledge to blend her structures into their natural settings.

B showing her how to make Native American drawings.

C allowing her to make some extra money along the way.

D keeping her from learning about more modern types of art.

10 **Which statement about Mary is supported by the text?**

F She was extremely well-known in her lifetime.

G She is extremely well-known today.

H She received prizes for her artistic and architectural work.

J She was responsible for designing famous buildings.

GO

How We Build

Directions: Here is an article about just a few of the building materials people use. Read the article, then do numbers 11–21.

Buildings can be made from many different materials, and the materials used will determine the structure's appearance. You have probably already seen some buildings made of the most common building materials, which are concrete, steel, brick, and wood.

Concrete is a mixture of portland cement, water, sand, and small stones. It is the most widely used building material in the world, and can be adapted to almost any shape. The greatest advantages of concrete are that it can be adapted to special needs, delivered to the work site in a semi-liquid state, and enhanced to make it more attractive.

Steel has been used in construction since the late 1880s. It is mostly seen in skyscrapers and bridges. Steel beams and rods are used in some kinds of construction that combine other materials, such as concrete or stone. In these cases, the steel reinforces the other materials and is not visible from the outside.

Bricks have been used in construction for a long time. Masons are the people who are trained to build things out of bricks and mortar, the substance that goes between the bricks. Most bricks are red, and the mortar is white or grey. The use of straight, squared forms gives brick structures a clean, ordered look. Bricks are also used for other structures, like chimneys, walls, and driveways.

Some of the first wooden houses in North America were rustic log cabins. In many parts of the country, wood is still the main building material for houses. Most wooden buildings have what is called a "frame" structure. Pieces of lumber are used to create a frame, then other materials are nailed in place to create the walls. Most houses made of wood are coated with one or more colors of paint for protection and decoration. They must be repainted once in a while, a process that is something of a nuisance but allows people to change the look of their houses.

Some types of structures, like tepees and igloos, are not permanent buildings. They are made from locally-available materials like sod (pieces of grass, roots

GO

and dirt), sticks, and snow. Though they may not look as sturdy as other structures, they provide effective shelter and warmth. In the case of a tepee, it can also be taken apart, moved, and rebuilt. This was an important feature for Plains Indians, who often moved to follow buffalo herds or for other reasons.

New building materials are being developed all the time. Some of these are made to be energy efficient or resistant to fire damage, while others use recycled products. The construction industry will continue to develop new materials, and with these changes, we can expect buildings to become better in a number of ways.

11 **This article is mostly about**

A different shapes of buildings.

B the reasons for building in a certain place.

C how people used to build their houses.

D different materials used for buildings.

12 **This article does *not* talk about**

F how buildings look.

G construction costs.

H movable buildings.

J what concrete is.

13 **Brick buildings are clean and ordered-looking because**

A they are usually straight and square.

B they are almost always red or brown.

C they have very high walls.

D they have very tall chimneys.

14 **A synonym for the word *enhance* is "improve." Which of these is an example of enhancing the appearance of concrete?**

F using too much water to weaken the concrete

G bringing the concrete to the work site

H adding stones to make the surface patterned

J using concrete around the world

15 **Which of these supports the idea that buildings will continue to look different in the future?**

A People will continue to build with wood.

B New building materials will be invented.

C Some people don't like the look of stone.

D Not everyone wants to live in a brick house.

GO

16 **Which of these would be another good title for this article?**

F *Careers in Building Construction*

G *More Than One Way to Build a House*

H *Building With Bricks and Mortar*

J *Construction Options and Costs*

17 **Which of these structures probably demands the most maintenance?**

A a house made of wood

B a building made of steel

C a house made of brick

D a building made of stone

18 **The author's purpose in writing the article was probably to report on**

F the cost of building materials.

G the increasing demand for brick.

H the decreasing interest in steel buildings.

J the great variety of building materials in use.

19 **According to the article, where would most steel buildings be found?**

A in areas where there are wooden buildings

B in areas where there are rock quarries

C in northern parts of the country

D in cities

20 **From evidence in the article, which of these descriptions best fits a building made of sod?**

F It blends into its setting and is not permanent.

G It contains steel beams and is not permanent.

H It is made of a combination of earth and straw.

J It is built with a "frame" structure.

21 **Here are two sentences related to the passage.**

Snow houses look cold from the outside.

They are warm on the inside.

Which of these best combines the two sentences into one?

A Although snow houses look cold from the outside, they are warm on the inside.

B Snow houses look cold; from the outside, they are warm on the inside.

C Snow houses look cold from the outside on the inside, they are warm.

D On the inside snow houses look warm, but they are cold from the outside.

GO

Directions: Here is a paragraph about a kind of work. Read the paragraph and choose the correct answer for 22 and 23.

_____. They work in various trades, such as plumbing, electricity, and woodworking. Each construction worker chooses a specialty and becomes better and better at that job. Some people decide to become master construction workers, or contractors. They must learn about all of the trades and be able to manage other people.

22 **Choose the best topic sentence for the paragraph.**

  F   To build your own house, you must have many skills.

  G   Contractors make sure buildings are finished on time.

  H   Construction workers are very talented people.

  J   Woodworking demands great care and skill.

23 **Which of these conclusions could be drawn from the paragraph?**

  A   Construction workers don't have much to learn.

  B   Managing people is a simple job.

  C   The only three trades are plumber, electrician, and woodworker.

  D   Contractors must understand each of the building trades.

STOP

Lesson 2 Reading Fiction

SAMPLE C

Archaeologists study the ruins of historical buildings. Some of the buildings are many thousands of years old. From their work, we can learn much about our past.

This story is mostly about

A an interesting career.

B becoming an archaeologist.

C ancient buildings.

D choosing a career.

TIPS

Skip difficult items and come back to them after you have tried the other items.

Think about what the author means as you read the story. This will help you answer the questions.

People often restore houses that have been lived in for years. The next story is about how a family helped to restore a house.

Directions: Read this story written by a boy who enjoys visiting his aunt, then do numbers 24–31.

Visiting Aunt Rita

My name is Lorenzo, and I want to tell you about a place I like. My Aunt Rita lives in an adobe house in a small New Mexico town. The house was built in 1890. Aunt Rita bought it a few years ago.

The reddish-brown house is two stories tall. It has five rooms, including a huge central dining room. When Aunt Rita bought the house, it needed a lot of work. My parents and I spent our summer vacation helping her. I did my part by tilling the garden and moving stones. When our work was finished, the house looked much better, and Aunt Rita was very grateful.

A couple of times a year, we drive to Aunt Rita's for a long weekend. I get to invite my best friend, Maggie. It takes a whole day to drive there. I like to watch the landscape change as we drive south into the high desert. When we drive up to the house, Aunt Rita comes out to greet us.

GO

There are always some chores to do during our visit, but they are different from the ones I do at home, so I don't mind doing them. My assignment is to help in the garden. Depending on the season, we either plant, maintain, or harvest vegetables. There isn't much weeding to do, since few weeds can survive at such a high elevation.

Maggie's job is to help chop and haul firewood. My dad taught her the safe way to use an ax. She piles firewood neatly by the back door, then brings some into the dining room. That way, Aunt Rita can start a fire in the kiva, a special rounded fireplace in the corner.

After our chores are finished, we go visiting. We have spent so much time at Aunt Rita's that Maggie and I have made many friends in the neighborhood. It's great to see them again, and each time we meet we have more and more fun.

In the evening, we prepare our meal. My favorite dinner is vegetable soup with fresh tortillas or bread. We always eat around an old wooden table, and we sit on a banco, a kind of built-in bench. We talk about our day and make plans for the next day. Time goes by quickly when we stay with Aunt Rita because we do many things that we don't get to do at home.

24 **Choose the sentence that best expresses what the passage is mostly about.**

   A Adobe houses are the best kinds of houses to live in.

   B Lorenzo likes spending time at his aunt's house.

   C Lorenzo is interested in building a house.

   D People should help each other and work together.

25 **Which of these pictures shows an activity described in the passage?**

F

G

H

J

GO

26 What is the major purpose of the story?

A to explain how to make something

B to tell how to get to a place

C to tell about an interesting place

D to argue for building with adobe

27 How does Lorenzo feel about his aunt's town now that he has been there many times?

F He is happy there, now more than ever.

G He likes it, but he wishes he had friends there.

H He sometimes wants to go somewhere else.

J He refuses to visit there from now on.

28 Why is Lorenzo so willing to help in the garden?

A He is afraid of disobeying his aunt.

G He isn't asked to work in the B at home.

C He wants to be the one to plant the vegetables.

D Gardening is one of his chores at home.

29 In the passage, Lorenzo's "assignment" is to help in the garden. The word "assignment" refers to

F how much you like to do something.

G something that can be planted.

H what you do after your chores are done.

J a task someone is asked to do.

30 Which of these actions shows that Lorenzo and his aunt like one another very much?

A He was greeted warmly when he arrived.

B He was asked to do work in the garden.

C He ate dinner at an old, wooden table.

D He had tortillas for dinner.

31 How are Lorenzo and Maggie similar?

F Both are asked to chop firewood.

G Both helped Aunt Rita fix up her house.

H Both are asked to weed the garden.

J Both made many new friends.

STOP

Lesson 3 Review

 SAMPLE D

Builders try to make windows and doors energy-efficient.

Which is the best way to write the sentence above?

A Energy-efficient windows and doors builders try.

B Builders, who try to make windows and doors energy-efficient.

C Builders trying to make windows and doors energy-efficient.

D Best as it is

Directions: The students in Mrs. Gonzaga's class are writing reports about building houses. Some students have decided to study parts that go into houses. Here is the first part of one student's report on windows.

[1] Windows are important parts of a house. [2] In all kinds of houses, windows providing light and ventilation. [3] They also allow us to see outside without opening doors. [4] Some windows are big and are intended to give us a nice view of the outdoors, small ones are mainly for letting fresh air in. [5] Some windows are just for decoration.

32 **Choose the best way to write Sentence 2.**

A In all kinds of houses, light and ventilation provided by windows.

B In all kinds of houses, windows provide light and ventilation.

C In all kinds of houses, windows to provide light and ventilation.

D Best as it is

33 **The sentence that should be written as two complete sentences is**

F Sentence 1

G Sentence 3

H Sentence 4

J Sentence 5

GO

Now read the second part of the report.

¹ In the past, before there were modern houses, people still needed windows. ² In rustic cabins, small windows were used to bring in fresh air. ³ People who built their houses out of earth made little open spaces in their walls. ⁴ These spaces created windows. ⁵ Until a few hundred years ago, windows were usually very small. ⁶ They didn't even have glass in them.

34 **Which of these best combines Sentences 3 and 4 into one?**

A People who built their houses out of earth made little open spaces in their walls to create windows.

B People who built their houses out of earth made little open spaces in their walls, these spaces created to be windows.

C People building their houses out of earth making little open spaces in their walls to create windows.

D Little open spaces in walls were created as windows in homes people were building out of earth.

35 **Select the best way to write Sentence 1.**

F In the past, people still needed windows before there were some modern houses.

G In the past, before modern houses were there, people still needed windows.

H Before there were modern houses in the past, people still need windows.

J Best as it is

GO

Here is the last part of the report.

¹ Today, new kinds of windows are available. ² Double-paned windows have two layers of glass. ³ These windows are energy-efficient, and can lower heating and cooling bills. ⁴ Some people buying architect-designed windows to make their houses look nice from the outside. ⁵ Very large windows are also available, these are most often seen on big, modern buildings.

36 What would be the best way to write Sentence 5?

A Very large windows also being available, and these are most often seen on big, modern buildings.

B Very large windows are also available. These windows are most often seen on big, modern buildings.

C Big, modern buildings are most often seen with the very large windows.

D Best as it is

37 Which shows the best way to write Sentence 4?

F Some people were buying architect-designed windows and were making their houses look nice from the outside.

G To make their houses look nice from the outside, some people had bought architect-designed windows.

H Some people buy architect-designed windows to make their houses look nice from the outside.

J Best as it is

38 Where would this sentence best fit in the paragraph?

Decorative windows come in many special shapes, including round.

A after Sentence 1   **C** after Sentence 3
B after Sentence 2   **D** after Sentence 4

STOP

Language Arts

Lesson 1 Vocabulary

Directions: For Sample A and numbers 1 and 2, read the sentences. Choose the word that correctly completes <u>both</u> sentences.

Directions: For Sample B and numbers 3 and 4, choose the word that means the <u>opposite</u> of the underlined word.

> **SAMPLE A**
>
> Choose the _____ number.
>
> It's _____ to see a purple dog.
>
> **A** even   **C** odd
>
> **B** unbelievable   **D** larger

> **SAMPLE B**
>
> omit information
>
> **F** include
> **H** examine
> **G** exclude
> **J** find

1 Did you _____ a room at the hotel?

The nature _____ is nearby.

A get   **C** area

B reserve   **D** request

2 My sister is playing on the _____.

_____ the bat carefully.

F slide   **H** step

G lift   **J** swing

3 <u>lush</u> jungle

A thick

B dark

C barren

D unexplored

4 <u>arrogant</u> comment

F vain

G thoughtful

H humorous

J modest

After you answer all the questions, check them one more time. Be sure your answers match the directions.

Stay with your first answer. Change it only if you are sure another one is better.

GO

Directions: For numbers 5–8, choose the word that means the same, or about the same, as the underlined word.

5 **make a pledge**

  A profit   **C** promise

  B trip   **D** comment

6 **visualize the scene**

  F forget   **H** imagine

  G enjoy   **J** recall

7 **precise measurement**

  A accurate   **C** approximate

  B incorrect   **D** unnecessary

8 **pleasant encounter**

  F entertainment   **H** weather

  G meeting   **J** vacation

Directions: For numbers 9–12, read the paragraph. For each numbered blank, there is a list of words with the same number. Choose the word from each list that best completes the meaning of the paragraph.

When most people think of __(9)__ Rome, they picture the remains of an empire that disappeared centuries ago. What they don't realize is that Rome has __(10)__ significantly to our civilization today. Our system of laws, for example, is based on Roman law. English, Spanish, French, and other languages contain many words of Roman __(11)__ . Even one of our most important building materials, concrete, was __(12)__ by the Romans.

9 **A** recent   **C** current

  B ancient   **D** immediate

10 **F** contributed   **H** updated

  G allowed   **J** adjusted

11 **A** termination   **C** origin

  B conflict   **D** extension

12 **F** misplaced   **H** preceded

  G established   **J** invented

STOP

Lesson 2 Language Mechanics

Directions: Choose the answer that is written correctly and shows the correct capitalization and punctuation.

SAMPLE C

A Yes? I will mow the lawn on Saturday.

B No, I don't mow the lawn in my sandals.

C Well I'm not sure we have enough gas.

D Yes I think we should be done by 3:00.

Keep in mind you are looking for correct capitalization and punctuation. Don't choose "Correct as it is" too often.

You may find it helpful to skim the item, then go over it again word by word.

Directions: For numbers 13–16, look at the underlined part of the sentence. Choose the answer that shows the best capitalization and punctuation for that part.

13 I went to the grocery store with my **grandmother. and** then we had lunch.

A grandmother and,

B grandmother; and

C grandmother, and

D Correct as it is

14 **Molly you,** really know how to dive well!

F Molly; you

G Molly, you

H Molly you

J Correct as it is

15 "Follow me," said **Bill, "and I** will show you the shortcut to my house."

A Bill, and"

B Bill, and

C Bill,"and

D Correct as it is

16 **Wev'e already** bought our new swimsuits.

F Weve' already

G Weve already

H We've already

J Correct as it is

GO

Directions: For numbers 17 and 18, choose the answer that is written correctly and shows the correct capitalization and punctuation.

17 **A** "I can't hear the news because you are talking," said Jon.

B "Oh, this is my favorite song"! said Paco

C "That radio doesn't work anymore," her father said

D Sally asked, "could you turn down the music please?"

18 **F** I memorized a poem called "The lily pad pond."

G We sang Home, Home on the Range in music class.

H *Outer Space* is a good book, but the library doesn't have it.

J The fifth chapter is titled the dinosaurs.

Directions: For numbers 19–22, read the story and the underlined parts. Choose the answer that shows the best capitalization and punctuation for each part.

Joey was busy working on his model
(19) <u>airplane it</u> had taken him all afternoon to paint the plane. Suddenly, he smelled something
(20) delicious and ran <u>downstairs. When</u> he reached
(21) the kitchen his father smiled at him and <u>said "I</u>
(22) knew it <u>would'nt</u> take you long to smell these cookies!"

19 **A** airplane, it
   B airplane: it
   C airplane. It
   D Correct as it is

20 **F** downstairs when
   G downstairs, when
   H Downstairs when
   J Correct as it is

21 **A** said, I
   B said, "I
   C said. "I
   D Correct as it is

22 **F** wouldn't
   G wouldnt'
   H wouldnt
   J Correct as it is

STOP

Lesson 3 Spelling

Directions: Find the underlined word that is **not** spelled correctly. If all of the underlined words are spelled correctly, mark "All correct."

SAMPLE D

A profitable <u>business</u>
B beautiful <u>region</u>
C earn a <u>commendation</u>
D <u>acquire</u> a horse
E All correct

Say each answer choice to yourself slowly and carefully while you look at it. Both senses will help you.

Don't spend too much time looking at the words. Pretty soon, they all begin to look like they are spelled wrong.

Directions: For numbers 23–25, choose the word that is spelled correctly and best completes the sentence.

23 **If we _____ we will win.**

A coperate   C coopperate
B cooperate   D coopirate

24 **A good scientist knows how to _____ natural events.**

F obsirve   H obscirve
G obzerve   J observe

25 **Tim made an _____ to his bicycle.**

A adjustment   C ajustmint
B ajustment   D adjustmine

Directions: For numbers 26 and 27, read each phrase. Find the underlined word that is **not** spelled correctly. If all the underlined words are spelled correctly, mark "All correct."

26 F brave <u>soldier</u>
G <u>victorious</u> team
H <u>selebrate</u> a holiday
J unusual <u>circumstances</u>
K All correct

27 A clever <u>disguise</u>
B make a <u>suggestion</u>
C <u>comparable</u> businesses
D helpful <u>attorney</u>
E All correct

STOP

Lesson 4 Writing

Directions: Read the short story below. Then write a few sentences to answer each question.

ALEX IN CHARGE

Alex was thrilled. Finally she was allowed to babysit her sister Connie by herself. Connie was four. When their parents left, Alex and Connie sat down to watch TV. "We're watching my show because I'm in charge," said Alex. Connie burst into tears, stood right in front of the TV, and wouldn't move. "Fine then. Let's eat. But we're eating what I want because I am in charge."

Alex microwaved the leftover macaroni and cheese and gave some to Connie. Connie dropped the bowl—upside down. "You did that on purpose!" said Alex. "You are going to bed right now because I am in charge!" She took a screaming Connie to the bedroom.

All of a sudden, Connie stopped crying. "What's that?" she said in a small, frightened voice. Alex listened and heard a strange noise. It sounded as if someone was climbing up the side of the house! Just then a huge, dark shadow fell across the room. Alex and Connie both screamed and held onto each other. They crept to the window in silence. They peered over the windowsill and saw a tree scratching against the pane. Sighing with relief, they fell onto Connie's bed, exhausted.

When their parents came home, they found Alex and Connie asleep with their arms around each other. "It's wonderful how the girls get along so well!" Mom said.

Tell about the main character in the story. _____

_____

_____

Explain the conflict in this story and how is it resolved. _____

_____

_____

How do Alex and Connie feel about each other? _____

_____

_____

GO

Directions: Should music be rated the same way movies are?
Write a short essay stating your opinion and why you think so.

_____

_____

_____

_____

_____

_____

_____

_____

_____

_____

_____

_____

_____

_____

_____

STOP

Lesson 5 Review

Directions: For Sample E and numbers 28–30, read the sentences. Choose the word that correctly completes **both** sentences.

SAMPLE
E

Put the salad in that _____.

I like to _____ on Wednesday.

  A plate   **C** golf
  B bowl   **D** container

28 How much water will that tank _____?

Please _____ the rope tightly.

  A contain   **C** release
  B grasp   **D** hold

29 We'll stop by _____ the game.

The children ran _____ each other.

  F after   **H** around
  G during   **J** over

30 Flowers are around the _____ of the pond.

We can _____ our way along the cliff.

  A side   **C** creep
  B edge   **D** border

Directions: For numbers 31 and 32, choose the word that means the **opposite** of the underlined word.

31 marvelous view

  F broad
  G narrow
  H exceptional
  J terrible

32 dilute the mixture

  A strengthen
  B weaken
  C enhance
  D analyze

Directions: For number 33, choose the word that means the same, or about the same, as the underlined word.

33 dispatch the workers

  F fire
  G pursue
  H send
  J educate

GO

Directions: For numbers 34 and 35, choose the answer that is written correctly and shows the correct capitalization and punctuation.

34 **A** "How many pages do you have left to read," asked Mina.

B Walker said "I have a three page report to write for homework."

C She asked? "Can I borrow these two books to read for my report."

D "I love to read adventure stories about mountain men," said Liam.

35 **F** Josephina who is a runner, trains six days a week.

G Sally, who is an artist has her own studio.

H My brother, who wants to be a teacher, is in college.

J Roberta who is a chef works very long hours.

Directions: For numbers 36–39, read the paragraph and the underlined parts. Choose the answer that shows the best capitalization and punctuation for each part.

(36)   Our town's <u>mayor Ann</u> Howard, is also a nurse. She has worked at the local
(37) <u>hospital, for</u> more than thirty years, but
(38) was elected mayor just last <u>year. When</u> asked why she was running for office, she
(39) <u>answered I</u> just couldn't stand to listen to people complain about the mayor."

36 **A** Mayor Ann **C** mayor, Ann
  B mayor ann, **D** Correct as it is

37 **F** hospital for **H** Hospital, for
  G hospital. For **J** Correct as it is

38 **A** year when **C** year when,
  B Year when **D** Correct as it is

39 **F** answered. "I **H** Answered, I
  G answered, "I **J** Correct as it is

GO

Directions: For numbers 40–43, choose the word that is spelled correctly and best completes the sentence.

40 **The new business made the town _____.**

A prosperous

B prosprous

C prosperus

D prospirous

41 **The weather is _____ here.**

F changeiable

G changeuble

H changeable

J changable

42 **Jets provide fast _____.**

A ocupation

B occupashun

C occupation

D okupation

43 **Vegetables are _____ foods.**

F nutrisious

G nutricus

H nootricious

J nutritious

Directions: For Sample F and numbers 44–47, read each phrase. Find the underlined word that is **not** spelled correctly. If all the underlined words are spelled correctly, mark "All correct."

 SAMPLE F

A create a budget

B castle guardian

C legendary explorer

D advertised price

E All correct

44 A comfortable shoes

B cool celar

C mentioned a name

D dangerous expedition

E All correct

45 F pleasant environment

G television antenna

H encourage students

J important equipment

K All correct

46 A solid evidence

B significant event

C important responsibility

D artificial flavors

E All correct

47 F beneficial class

G carnivorous animal

H difficult decision

J business conferance

K All correct

STOP

Directions: Choose one historical figure you would like to have known. Write three or four paragraphs explaining why you chose this person.

_____

_____

_____

_____

_____

_____

_____

_____

_____

_____

_____

_____

_____

_____

_____

_____

_____

_____

_____

STOP

Mathematics

Lesson 1 Computation

SAMPLE A

$5 \times (7 + 2) =$

A 37
B 45
C 70
D 14
E None of these

SAMPLE B

$6.4 \div 0.8 =$

F 0.08
G 0.8
H 800
J 80
K None of these

Look at each problem carefully. Pay attention to decimals, fractions, operation signs, and the order of operations.

Check your answer by either using the opposite operation or repeating the solution of the problem.

1 $29.23 + 6.5 =$

A 29.88
B 22.73
C 94.23
D 35.73
E None of these

3 30% of 45 =

A 1.5
B 12.5
C 13.5
D 135
E None of these

2 $^-48 + 9 =$

F $^-39$
G 39
H $^-37$
J $^-57$
K None of these

4 $\frac{5}{6} \div \frac{6}{11} =$

F $\frac{5}{11}$
G $\frac{1}{6}$
H $\frac{8}{11}$
J $1\frac{19}{36}$
K None of these

STOP

Lesson 2 Mathematics Skills

SAMPLE C **The quadrilateral has been flipped over the dashed line.**

What are the coordinates of the covered vertex?

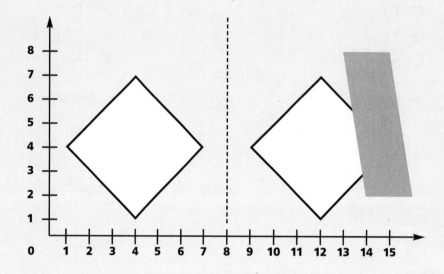

A (14, 4)

B (15, 4)

C (14, 3)

D (16, 4)

- Try the easiest items first.

- Eliminate answers that can't be right.

- If a question sounds difficult, try saying it to yourself in a way you can understand.

GO

5 What number is missing from this number sequence?

356, _____, 368, 374

A 362
B 364
C 366
D 367

6 Lamia entered a number into a calculator.
Then she pressed these keys:

When she finished, the calculator showed 13.
What was the number that Lamia started with?

F 32
G 12
H 20
J 24

7 What is the probability that this spinner will stop on 2?

A $\frac{1}{4}$
B $\frac{1}{3}$
C $\frac{1}{2}$
D 1

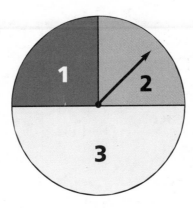

GO

8 **Look at the picture of Bobby reading the thermometer. What was the temperature at 8 A.M.?**

F ⁻10 degrees F

G ⁻8 degrees F

H ⁻4 degrees F

J 24 degrees F

"Mom, it's 11:00 A.M., and it is already 14 degrees warmer than it was at 8:00 A.M."

9 **What are all the factors of 24?**

A 2, 3, 6, 12

B 1, 3, 4, 12

C 1, 2, 3, 4, 12, 24

D 1, 2, 3, 4, 6, 8, 12, 24

10 **Which of these number sentences is false?**

F 8.65 > 8.56

G 1.89 > 1.98

J 5.65 > 5.56

H 3.87 > 3.78

11 $p + p + p + q = 21$

$q + q = 12$

In the problem above, each letter represents a certain number. What number does the letter *p* represent?

A 4   C 6

B 5   D 7

12 **Jeremy's average on his first 7 math quizzes was 86.429. What is the place value of the 9 in his average?**

F tens   H hundredths

G thousands   J thousandths

GO

HALLOWEEN PARTY

Directions: Jessica and her parents are planning a Halloween party. Do numbers 13–18 about the party.

13 Jessica's mother made apple pies for all 29 people. The picture shows the part of a whole apple pie each person will get. How many whole pies does she have to make?

   A 2
   B 3
   C 4
   D 5

14 Jessica's father spilled some punch on the tiled countertop. Estimate the number of tiles covered by the punch.

   F 2
   G 4
   H 8
   J 10

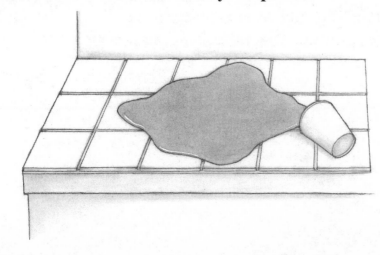

GO

15 The perimeter of the room in which the party will take place is 70 feet. The width is 15 feet. What is the length?

A 40 feet   **C** 20 feet

B 30 feet   **D** 10 feet

16 Five people will be assigned to each tub when they bob for apples. How many tubs of apples will a group of 29 people need?

F 3   **H** 5

G 4   **J** 6

17 Jessica discovered that she could cut out four ghosts at a time if she folded the white paper in half and then folded it in half again before cutting. What were the measurements of the folded paper from which she cut the ghosts?

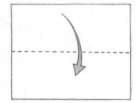 

A $5\frac{1}{2}$ inches × $8\frac{1}{2}$ inches   **C** 11 inches × $4\frac{1}{2}$ inches

B $5\frac{1}{2}$ inches × $4\frac{1}{4}$ inches   **D** 11 inches by $8\frac{1}{4}$ inches

18 Jessica cut out pumpkins for decorations.
Which shape was cut from the folded piece of paper?

   **F**   **G**   **H**    **J**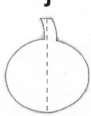

STOP

Lesson 3 Review

SAMPLE
D

70% of 52 =

A 36.4
B 35.0
C 3.5
D 3.64
E None of these

SAMPLE
E

$7 \times 9 + (12 \div 3) =$

F 25
G 91
H 67
J 252
K None of these

19
564.4
– 0.6

A 565
B 564.8
C 563.8
D 563.6
E None of these

22 $^-4 \times {}^-8 =$

F $^-32$
G $^-12$
H 34
J 4
K None of these

20 $6.5 \times 5.6 =$

F 35.4
G 64
H 3640
J 36.1
K None of these

23 $\frac{8}{25} = \frac{n}{100}$

n =

A 16
B 32
C 4
D 50
E None of these

21 $3\frac{5}{6} - \frac{1}{5} =$

A $3\frac{19}{30}$
B 4
C $3\frac{3}{10}$
D $4\frac{1}{30}$
E None of these

24 $\frac{7}{9}$ $+\frac{2}{3}$

F $\frac{9}{12}$
G $1\frac{5}{9}$
H $\frac{4}{9}$
J $1\frac{4}{9}$
K None of these

GO

SAMPLE F **Which sign can go in the squares to make the number sentence true?**

9 □ (3 □ 5) = (9 □ 3) □ 5

A >

B ÷

C −

D +

25 **Fido and Lassie are facing each other. Which picture shows the dogs' positions after Fido turns 360 degrees and Lassie turns 180 degrees?**

Fido   **Lassie**

A

B

C

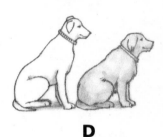

D

26 **Miko sorted these polygons into two groups. Which of these rules could she have used to sort the polygons?**

F   All regular polygons belong in Group I.

G   All figures with an obtuse angle belong in Group II.

H   All figures with an even number of sides belong in Group I.

J   All equiangular figures belong in Group II.

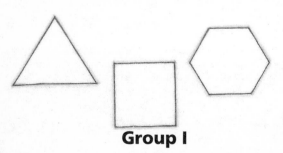

Group I

Group II

GO

Game Show

Directions: The seventh grade class at Murray Hill School is going to a screening of a family game show. Do numbers 27–30 about the show.

27 Kim, Nicole, Ryan, and Rose were a team in the puzzle part of the show, in which each child had to put together a five-piece puzzle. The team's total time was 85.2 seconds. What was Rose's time?

Name	Time
Kim	21.8 seconds
Nicole	18.9 seconds
Ryan	24.6 seconds
Rose	

A 20.9 seconds

B 29.9 seconds

C 18.9 seconds

D 30.9 seconds

E None of these

28 Quentin completed a 50-foot obstacle course in 30 seconds. At this rate, how long would it take him to complete an 80-foot obstacle course?

F 48 seconds

G 60 seconds

H 80 seconds

J 110 seconds

K None of these

29 The students could buy pretzels at the game show. Miguel bought $3\frac{1}{2}$ pounds of pretzels at $1.20 per pound. How much did he pay for the pretzels?

A $0.42

B $1.42

C $4.20

D $42.00

E None of these

30 The students went by van to the game show. Each van can hold 12 students. They completely filled 8 vans. How many students went to the game show?

F 20

G 96

H 100

J 120

K None of these

GO

TAKE THE TRAIN

Directions: Amanda travels 60 minutes to work by train. She takes one train from Middlebury to Southbury, where she catches a second train for Oxford. The graph shows the distance she has traveled each time. Use the graph to do numbers 31–33.

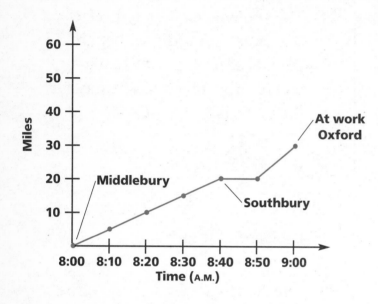

31 **At what time is Amanda waiting for her second train?**

A 8:10 A.M. to 8:20 A.M.   **C** 8:40 A.M. to 8:50 A.M.

B 8:20 A.M. to 8:40 A.M.   **D** 8:50 A.M. to 9:00 A.M.

32 **How many miles does she travel by 8:30?**

F 5 miles   **H** 15 miles

G 10 miles   **J** 20 miles

33 **At what time does Amanda travel at the greatest speed?**

A 8:10 A.M. to 8:20 A.M.   **C** 8:40 A.M. to 8:50 A.M.

B 8:20 A.M. to 8:40 A.M.   **D** 8:50 A.M. to 9:00 A.M.

STOP

Lesson 1

Directions: For numbers 1–8, choose the correct answer.

1 The Pax Romana began with Augustus. *Pax Romana* means

   A Precision of Rome.
   B Roman Peace.
   C Proximity of Rome.
   D Romano Pride.

2 When Rome became an empire, its days as a _____ came to an end.

   F state
   G city
   H republic
   J dynasty

3 Who was the first Roman emperor?

   A Caligula
   B Tiberius
   C Nero
   D Augustus

4 Rome is the capital city of what country?

   F Egypt
   G Italy
   H Israel
   J Greece

5 Which of the following was not a reform introduced by Augustus?

   A reorganizing the army
   B building large residences
   C setting a census
   D creating a strong civil service

6 Who is credited with first stating that Earth turns on its axis once every twenty-four hours?

   F Montesquieu
   G Copernicus
   H Voltaire
   J Aristotle

7 Newton is famous for having written his law of

   A conduct.
   B planets.
   C gravity.
   D nobility.

8 Who invented movable type in 1447?

   F Samuel F. B. Morse
   G Benjamin Franklin
   H Thomas Edison
   J Johannes Gutenberg

GO

Directions: For numbers 9–15, choose the correct answer.

9 Suppose that you have been assigned a detailed report on a Mali ruler. Which of these reference materials would be least helpful?

A Internet

B encyclopedia

C dictionary

D biography

10 In medieval England, *chivalry* could best be described as

F a conduct code for knights.

G a form of horse racing.

H an organizational tool for farming.

J a way of introducing kings and queens.

11 Which of these poets wrote in medieval Europe?

A Dante

B Longfellow

C Sappho

D Kalidasa

12 In medieval Europe, vassals worked the land belonging to

F a queen.

G a lord.

H a peasant.

J a farmer.

13 Which of the following statements about the church in medieval Europe is true?

A Church authority was not questioned.

B Ancient knowledge was rejected by the Church.

C The Church was closely linked to feudal society.

D The Church worked to spur on feudal warfare.

14 Which of the following locations was not a site of early Andean civilization?

F Argentina

G Mexico

H Paraguay

J Chile

15 The Andean civilization existed during the

A sixteenth century.

B seventeenth century.

C eighteenth century.

D nineteenth century.

STOP

Lesson 2 Review

Directions: Study the time line that shows important events in Muhammad's life, and then do numbers 16–18.

Muhammad's Life

Muhammad, also known as the Prophet of Islam, is born in Mecca.	Learning of a plan to murder him, Muhammad escapes with his followers to Yathrib. This year becomes the first year of the Muslim calendar. Muhammad's daughter, Fatima, dies.	Muhammad returns to Mecca with the *Koran*, the holy book of Islam.	Muhammad conquers Mecca. He claims all of Arabia.	Muhammad dies.
570	622	629	630	632

16 **Which of the following events happened first?**

F The Prophet of Islam died.

G Muhammad conquered Mecca.

H the first year of the Muslim calendar

J Muhammad took the *Koran* to Mecca.

17 **When did Muhammad claim all of Arabia?**

A after his daughter died

B before he learned of a plan to murder him

C while he was in Yathrib

D during the first year of the Muslim calendar

18 **Which of these events happened two years apart?**

F Muhammad's daughter died.
Muhammad claimed all of Arabia.

G The Prophet of Islam was born.
The first year of the Muslim calendar came into existence.

H Muhammad took the *Koran* to Mecca.
Muhammad escaped with his followers to Yathrib.

J Muhammad conquered Mecca.
Muhammad died.

GO

Directions: In the chart below, some of the accomplishments of famous Renaissance personalities are listed. For numbers 19–22, read the chart and answer the questions that follow.

Name	Gained Fame as	Example of Accomplishments	Type of Work
Michelangelo Buonarroti	artist/sculptor	Pietà	sculpture
François Rabelais	author	Gargantua et Pantagruel	book
Leonardo da Vinci	artist/inventor	Mona Lisa	painting
Miguel de Cervantes	author	Don Quixote	book
Giovanni Boccaccio	author	Decameron	book
Raphael Santi	artist	Baldassare Castiglione	painting
Donatello	artist/sculptor	David	sculpture
Sir Thomas More	author/statesman	Utopia	book
William Shakespeare	poet/playwright	Romeo and Juliet	play

19 The chart tells you that _____ was an inventor.

A Sir Thomas More

B Leonardo da Vinci

C William Shakespeare

D Michelangelo Buonarroti

20 Who gained fame as the author of *Don Quixote?*

F Donatello

G Raphael Santi

H Miguel de Cervantes

J François Rabelais

21 Decameron is a _____.

A book

B painting

C play

D sculpture

22 Sculptures are listed as accomplishments for two people. These people are

F Donatello and François Rabelais.

G Miguel de Cervantes and Raphael Santi.

H Sir Thomas More and Giovanni Boccaccio.

J Michelangelo Buonarroti and Donatello.

STOP

Lesson 1

Directions: For numbers 1 and 2, read the passage and answer the questions that follow.

Supercontinent Pangaea

Have you ever noticed how South America and Africa seem to fit together? Scientists believe that 200 million years ago the Earth's continents were joined together to form one gigantic supercontinent called Pangaea. As the rock plates that the continents sit on moved, the supercontinent broke up and moved apart.

One piece of evidence to support this theory is the fact that the shapes of the continents match. For example, the bulge of Africa fits the shape of the coast of North America, while Brazil fits along the coast of Africa beneath the bulge. There is also evidence from plant fossils of late Paleozoic age. Fossils found on several different continents were quite similar. This suggests that they evolved together on a single large landmass. Geologists have also found that broad belts of rocks in Africa and South America are the same type. These broad belts then match when the ends of the continents are joined.

This "continental drift" is far from over. The Earth's crust is constantly moving at rates of up to several inches a year. A widely-held theory that explains these movements is called plate tectonics. The term plate refers to large rigid blocks of Earth's surface, which appear to move as a unit. These plates may include both oceans and continents. When the plates move, the continents and ocean floor above them move as well. Continental drift occurs when the continents change position in relation to each other.

1 Evidence supporting continental drift includes all except which of the following?

A The shapes of the continents fit together.

B Fossils from different continents are alike.

C Animals in Africa and North America are similar today.

D Rocks from different continents are of the same type.

2 Which best summarizes the theory of plate tectonics?

F It explains why certain plant fossils were formed during the Paleozoic age.

G It explains how changes in Earth's crust are due to the movement of large blocks of Earth's surface.

H It explains why the continents are shifting to eventually form a supercontinent which will be called Pangaea.

J It explains why dinner plates are named after parts of Earth's crust.

GO

Directions: For numbers 3–5, use the passage to choose the correct answer.

Scott's Experiment

After discovering a moldy loaf of bread in a kitchen cabinet, Scott decided to do an experiment to determine the conditions under which mold grows the best. He suspected that mold grows best in the dark, so he put his idea to the test.

Scott bought a new loaf of bread and some sandwich bags. In each bag, he put a slice of bread, a damp paper towel, and a bit of soil. He put the bags in places that receive different amounts of light, but would remain at room temperature.

In three days, Scott checked the bags. He found the most mold growing on the bread that he had put in a dark place.

3 **What was Scott's hypothesis?**

A Mold grows best in a sandwich bag.

B Mold will take over the world in the year 2009.

C Mold grows best in the dark.

D Mold grows best at room temperature.

4 **What was the dependent variable in Scott's experiment?**

F the bread

G the amount of light

H the temperature

J the moisture

5 **Scott came up with a hypothesis, then tested it. Scott used the**

A scientific method.

B decomposer.

C encyclopedia.

D physical change.

Directions: For numbers 6 and 7, choose the correct answer.

6 **When Michele added a clear liquid to a test tube full of blue liquid, the liquid in the test tube turned red. This is an example of a**

F prediction.   **G** physical change.   **H** chemical change.   **J** variable.

7 **Which of the following is a producer?**

A an orangutan   **B** a sparrow   **C** a comet   **D** a daisy

STOP

Lesson 2 Review

Directions: For numbers 8–15, choose the correct answer.

8 The smallest amount of an element that still maintains all the properties of that element is called

F an atom.

G a nucleus.

H a molecule.

J a compound.

9 Which of the following would you not expect to find in a desert ecosystem?

A succulent plants

B symbiotic relationships between animals

C seasons

D trees that change colors in fall

10 Which of the following is the chemical symbol for water?

F H_2O

G O_2

H CO_2

J N

11 Which of these tools would be best to measure the volume of a liquid?

A thermometer

B balance scale

C graduated cylinder

D barometer

12 When water freezes, it

F expands.

G vaporizes.

H contracts.

J radiates.

13 When water changes to a gas, it is called

A expansion.

B erosion.

C evaporation.

D pollution.

14 The system of the human body which takes in oxygen and expels carbon dioxide is called the

F circulatory system.

G respiratory system.

H nervous system.

J digestive system.

15 A doctor who treats people with heart problems is

A a radiologist.

B a dermatologist.

C a cardiologist.

D an oncologist.

GO

Directions: Use the information from the graph to answer numbers 16–20.

Anthony did an experiment to see how the flight of a paper airplane would be affected by changing the angle of the airplane's wings. He constructed three paper airplanes, slanting the wings down on Plane 1, and slanting them up on Plane 2. The wings of Plane 3 were level.

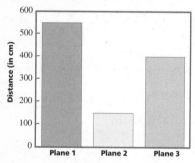

16 Anthony might have decided to make a graph because it made it easier to

F keep his data organized.

G compare the distances each plane flew.

H draw conclusions about his data.

J all of the above

17 The dependent variable in Anthony's experiment was the

A paper that he used to build the airplanes.

B angle of the airplane's wings.

C size of the airplane.

D weight that he put on the nose of the airplane.

18 Which of the following conclusions can Anthony draw from the graph?

F Paper airplanes fly best with their wings pointed up.

G Paper airplanes fly best with level wings.

H Paper airplanes fly best with their wings pointed down.

J Real airplanes fly best with level wings.

19 Which of the following statements is not true?

A Plane 1 flew more than twice as far as Plane 2.

B Plane 3 flew half as far as Plane 1.

C Plane 2 flew 400 centimeters less than Plane 1.

D Plane 2 flew less than half as far as Plane 3.

20 Plane 1 flew an average of 550 centimeters. If Anthony wanted to compare the distances that Plane 1 flew during each flight, what would be the best graphic to use?

F a bar graph

G a pictograph

H a pie chart

J a double line graph

STOP

Final Test Answer Sheet

Fill in only one letter for each item. If you change an answer, make sure to erase your first mark completely.

Unit 1: Reading, pages 125–130

A Ⓐ Ⓑ Ⓒ Ⓓ	**7** Ⓐ Ⓑ Ⓒ Ⓓ	**14** Ⓕ Ⓖ Ⓗ Ⓙ	**21** Ⓕ Ⓖ Ⓗ Ⓙ	**28** Ⓕ Ⓖ Ⓗ Ⓙ
1 Ⓐ Ⓑ Ⓒ Ⓓ	**8** Ⓕ Ⓖ Ⓗ Ⓙ	**15** Ⓐ Ⓑ Ⓒ Ⓓ	**22** Ⓕ Ⓖ Ⓗ Ⓙ	**29** Ⓕ Ⓖ Ⓗ Ⓙ
2 Ⓕ Ⓖ Ⓗ Ⓙ	**9** Ⓐ Ⓑ Ⓒ Ⓓ	**16** Ⓕ Ⓖ Ⓗ Ⓙ	**23** Ⓕ Ⓖ Ⓗ Ⓙ	**30** Ⓕ Ⓖ Ⓗ Ⓙ
3 Ⓐ Ⓑ Ⓒ Ⓓ	**10** Ⓕ Ⓖ Ⓗ Ⓙ	**17** Ⓐ Ⓑ Ⓒ Ⓓ	**24** Ⓐ Ⓑ Ⓒ Ⓓ	**31** Ⓕ Ⓖ Ⓗ Ⓙ
4 Ⓕ Ⓖ Ⓗ Ⓙ	**11** Ⓐ Ⓑ Ⓒ Ⓓ	**18** Ⓕ Ⓖ Ⓗ Ⓙ	**25** Ⓐ Ⓑ Ⓒ Ⓓ	
5 Ⓐ Ⓑ Ⓒ Ⓓ	**12** Ⓕ Ⓖ Ⓗ Ⓙ	**19** Ⓐ Ⓑ Ⓒ Ⓓ	**26** Ⓐ Ⓑ Ⓒ Ⓓ	
6 Ⓕ Ⓖ Ⓗ Ⓙ	**13** Ⓐ Ⓑ Ⓒ Ⓓ	**20** Ⓕ Ⓖ Ⓗ Ⓙ	**27** Ⓐ Ⓑ Ⓒ Ⓓ	

Unit 2: Language Arts, pages 131–137

A Ⓐ Ⓑ Ⓒ Ⓓ	**11** Ⓐ Ⓑ Ⓒ Ⓓ	**21** Ⓐ Ⓑ Ⓒ Ⓓ	**32** Ⓕ Ⓖ Ⓗ Ⓙ	**43** Ⓐ Ⓑ Ⓒ Ⓓ
1 Ⓐ Ⓑ Ⓒ Ⓓ	**12** Ⓕ Ⓖ Ⓗ Ⓙ	**22** Ⓕ Ⓖ Ⓗ Ⓙ	**33** Ⓐ Ⓑ Ⓒ Ⓓ	**44** Ⓕ Ⓖ Ⓗ Ⓙ
2 Ⓕ Ⓖ Ⓗ Ⓙ	**B** Ⓐ Ⓑ Ⓒ Ⓓ	**23** Ⓐ Ⓑ Ⓒ Ⓓ	**34** Ⓕ Ⓖ Ⓗ Ⓙ	**45** Ⓐ Ⓑ Ⓒ Ⓓ
3 Ⓐ Ⓑ Ⓒ Ⓓ	**13** Ⓐ Ⓑ Ⓒ Ⓓ	**24** Ⓕ Ⓖ Ⓗ Ⓙ	**35** Ⓐ Ⓑ Ⓒ Ⓓ	**46** Ⓕ Ⓖ Ⓗ Ⓙ
4 Ⓕ Ⓖ Ⓗ Ⓙ	**14** Ⓕ Ⓖ Ⓗ Ⓙ	**25** Ⓐ Ⓑ Ⓒ Ⓓ	**36** Ⓕ Ⓖ Ⓗ Ⓙ	**47** Ⓐ Ⓑ Ⓒ Ⓓ
5 Ⓐ Ⓑ Ⓒ Ⓓ	**15** Ⓐ Ⓑ Ⓒ Ⓓ	**26** Ⓕ Ⓖ Ⓗ Ⓙ	**37** Ⓐ Ⓑ Ⓒ Ⓓ	**48** Ⓕ Ⓖ Ⓗ Ⓙ
6 Ⓕ Ⓖ Ⓗ Ⓙ	**16** Ⓕ Ⓖ Ⓗ Ⓙ	**27** Ⓐ Ⓑ Ⓒ Ⓓ	**38** Ⓕ Ⓖ Ⓗ Ⓙ	**49** Ⓐ Ⓑ Ⓒ Ⓓ
7 Ⓐ Ⓑ Ⓒ Ⓓ	**17** Ⓐ Ⓑ Ⓒ Ⓓ Ⓔ	**28** Ⓕ Ⓖ Ⓗ Ⓙ	**39** Ⓐ Ⓑ Ⓒ Ⓓ	
8 Ⓕ Ⓖ Ⓗ Ⓙ	**18** Ⓕ Ⓖ Ⓗ Ⓙ Ⓚ	**29** Ⓐ Ⓑ Ⓒ Ⓓ	**40** Ⓕ Ⓖ Ⓗ Ⓙ	
9 Ⓐ Ⓑ Ⓒ Ⓓ	**19** Ⓐ Ⓑ Ⓒ Ⓓ Ⓔ	**30** Ⓕ Ⓖ Ⓗ Ⓙ	**41** Ⓐ Ⓑ Ⓒ Ⓓ	
10 Ⓕ Ⓖ Ⓗ Ⓙ	**20** Ⓕ Ⓖ Ⓗ Ⓙ Ⓚ	**31** Ⓐ Ⓑ Ⓒ Ⓓ	**42** Ⓕ Ⓖ Ⓗ Ⓙ	

Final Test Answer Sheet

Unit 3: Mathematics, pages 140–148

A Ⓐ Ⓑ Ⓒ Ⓓ Ⓔ   7 Ⓐ Ⓑ Ⓒ Ⓓ   16 Ⓕ Ⓖ Ⓗ Ⓙ   25 Ⓐ Ⓑ Ⓒ Ⓓ   34 Ⓕ Ⓖ Ⓗ Ⓙ

B Ⓕ Ⓖ Ⓗ Ⓙ Ⓚ   8 Ⓕ Ⓖ Ⓗ Ⓙ   17 Ⓐ Ⓑ Ⓒ Ⓓ   26 Ⓕ Ⓖ Ⓗ Ⓙ   35 Ⓐ Ⓑ Ⓒ Ⓓ

1 Ⓐ Ⓑ Ⓒ Ⓓ Ⓔ   9 Ⓐ Ⓑ Ⓒ Ⓓ   18 Ⓕ Ⓖ Ⓗ Ⓙ   27 Ⓐ Ⓑ Ⓒ Ⓓ   36 Ⓕ Ⓖ Ⓗ Ⓙ

2 Ⓕ Ⓖ Ⓗ Ⓙ Ⓚ   10 Ⓕ Ⓖ Ⓗ Ⓙ   19 Ⓐ Ⓑ Ⓒ Ⓓ   28 Ⓕ Ⓖ Ⓗ Ⓙ   37 Ⓐ Ⓑ Ⓒ Ⓓ

3 Ⓐ Ⓑ Ⓒ Ⓓ Ⓔ   11 Ⓐ Ⓑ Ⓒ Ⓓ   20 Ⓕ Ⓖ Ⓗ Ⓙ   29 Ⓐ Ⓑ Ⓒ Ⓓ   38 Ⓕ Ⓖ Ⓗ Ⓙ

4 Ⓕ Ⓖ Ⓗ Ⓙ Ⓚ   12 Ⓕ Ⓖ Ⓗ Ⓙ   21 Ⓐ Ⓑ Ⓒ Ⓓ   30 Ⓕ Ⓖ Ⓗ Ⓙ   39 Ⓐ Ⓑ Ⓒ Ⓓ

5 Ⓐ Ⓑ Ⓒ Ⓓ Ⓔ   13 Ⓐ Ⓑ Ⓒ Ⓓ   22 Ⓕ Ⓖ Ⓗ Ⓙ   31 Ⓐ Ⓑ Ⓒ Ⓓ   40 Ⓕ Ⓖ Ⓗ Ⓙ

6 Ⓕ Ⓖ Ⓗ Ⓙ Ⓚ   14 Ⓕ Ⓖ Ⓗ Ⓙ   23 Ⓐ Ⓑ Ⓒ Ⓓ   32 Ⓕ Ⓖ Ⓗ Ⓙ   41 Ⓐ Ⓑ Ⓒ Ⓓ

C Ⓐ Ⓑ Ⓒ Ⓓ   15 Ⓐ Ⓑ Ⓒ Ⓓ   24 Ⓕ Ⓖ Ⓗ Ⓙ   33 Ⓐ Ⓑ Ⓒ Ⓓ

Unit 4: Social Studies, pages 149–150

1 Ⓐ Ⓑ Ⓒ Ⓓ   6 Ⓕ Ⓖ Ⓗ Ⓙ

2 Ⓕ Ⓖ Ⓗ Ⓙ   7 Ⓐ Ⓑ Ⓒ Ⓓ

3 Ⓐ Ⓑ Ⓒ Ⓓ   8 Ⓕ Ⓖ Ⓗ Ⓙ

4 Ⓕ Ⓖ Ⓗ Ⓙ   9 Ⓐ Ⓑ Ⓒ Ⓓ

5 Ⓐ Ⓑ Ⓒ Ⓓ

Unit 5: Science, pages 151–152

1 Ⓐ Ⓑ Ⓒ Ⓓ   5 Ⓐ Ⓑ Ⓒ Ⓓ   9 Ⓐ Ⓑ Ⓒ Ⓓ

2 Ⓕ Ⓖ Ⓗ Ⓙ   6 Ⓕ Ⓖ Ⓗ Ⓙ   10 Ⓕ Ⓖ Ⓗ Ⓙ

3 Ⓐ Ⓑ Ⓒ Ⓓ   7 Ⓐ Ⓑ Ⓒ Ⓓ

4 Ⓕ Ⓖ Ⓗ Ⓙ   8 Ⓕ Ⓖ Ⓗ Ⓙ

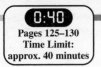

Pages 125–130
Time Limit:
approx. 40 minutes

SAMPLE A

Nick really liked his grandfather, but had a hard time talking to him. His grandfather was from Italy, and Nick didn't know Italian. One day, Nick thought of a simple way to solve the problem.

Which of these is probably Nick's solution?

A move to Italy and learn Italian

B have Grandfather teach him Italian

C teach Grandfather how to type

D spend less time with Grandfather

Directions: Many people today are interested in discovering their family histories. This is the story of a girl who is taking the first step in this direction. Read the story, then do numbers 1–9.

Family Tree

"How did Grandma and Grandpa meet each other, Mom?" asked Sonia.

"I didn't know you were interested in that old stuff," her mother replied, smiling. "Well, they met in 1936. They helped out on the same farm after school. Grandma didn't have many friends at the time."

"What were Grandma's mother and father named?" asked Sonia.

"Their names were Regina and Gerald Hellstern," said her mother. "Gerald was the first person in his whole family to be born outside of Germany. That was back in 1885."

Sonia was impressed. "Wow, that was a long time ago. How do you know this stuff?"

"For the past few years, your uncle and I have been researching our family history," her mother answered. "We have reconstructed a family tree that goes all the way back to 1749."

"A family tree? What kind of tree is that?" asked Sonia, getting a little confused.

"It's not a real tree, honey," was the answer. "Here, look at this." Sonia watched as her mother drew lines and wrote names on a piece of paper. She told Sonia a few stories about her ancestors. Sonia was amazed at how interesting their lives were.

"Please tell me another one," Sonia pleaded.

GO

1 Some of Sonia's ancestors were from what country?

A Mexico

B Italy

C Germany

D England

2 Sonia's great-grandfather was the first person in his family to

F leave Germany.

G be born in the United States.

H be born in Germany.

J work on a farm after school.

3 Which person from the story is shown in the illustration on this page?

A Sonia

B Sonia's mother

C Sonia's grandmother

D Sonia's great-grandmother

4 Sonia's mother probably hadn't told her daughter the family histories sooner because

F family histories are really only for adults.

G she thought the stories were too sad to tell.

H Sonia was much too young to hear about it.

J she didn't know Sonia wanted to hear them.

5 The story is about a girl who

A just became interested in her family's past.

B just moved to the United States from Europe.

C works on a farm with her mother.

D has studied her family tree for a long time.

GO

6 **Choose the sentence that is complete and written correctly.**

    F Sonia's mother proud that her daughter wants to learn.

    G Sonia liking to hear her mother's stories.

    H Sonia learned that a family tree wasn't a real tree.

    J Told that many of her ancestors had difficult lives.

7 **Sonia probably will**

    A hear more stories about her ancestors.

    B quickly grow tired of listening to stories.

    C write a letter to her grandparents.

    D call her uncle to ask him to tell some stories.

8 **Which statement about Sonia is supported by the text?**

    F She is not very interested in past events.

    G She likes to hear made-up stories.

    H She is mainly interested in herself.

    J She likes to learn new things.

9 **Choose the sentence that best combines these sentences into one.**

Sonia's grandmother met her future husband in 1936.

She was working on a farm when she met him.

She didn't have many friends when she met him.

    A In 1936, Sonia's grandmother met her future husband when she was working on a farm and didn't have many friends.

    B Sonia's grandmother, working on a farm, met her future husband in 1936 and didn't have many friends.

    C Not having many friends, in 1936, Sonia's grandmother met her future husband when she was working on a farm.

    D Sonia's grandmother met her future husband in 1936, when she was working on a farm, although she didn't have many friends.

GO

Directions: Use this campus map to do numbers 10 and 11.

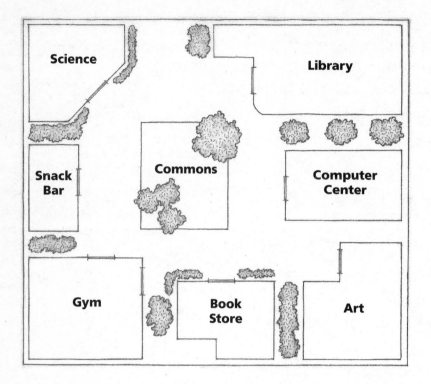

10 **Which of these can be determined from the information on the map?**

   F   how many students are in each building

   G   how to find a building on campus

   H   what time the classes start and stop

   J   who designed the college campus

11 **Imagine that you are in the Art building and someone asks you how to get to the Science building. Which of the following would direct the person correctly?**

   A   Go out the door, turn right, pass the Computer Center, and walk straight ahead.

   B   Go out the door, walk to the Gym, then turn right.

   C   Leave the Art building, then turn left at the Book Store.

   D   Go out the door, turn right, and turn right again at the Library.

GO

Directions: Read the passage. Then answer the questions.

Storm Chaser

Oklahoman Warren Faidley has a job most people think is exciting, but one not many would want; he is a tornado chaser. Ordinary people take shelter when a storm approaches, but Faidley does just the opposite. He grabs his camera, computer, and other equipment and follows the funnel. Faidley is also a writer and a speaker, and has even worked on a movie about tornadoes as a technical consultant.

Tornado season in the Southwest lasts from mid-April until June. Faidley spends that time in the Texas-Oklahoma-Kansas-Missouri area where tornadoes are more likely to appear. In the "off season," he lives in Arizona, writing about storms and speaking to various groups.

Faidley says he is not a daredevil, and he has grown even more cautious as he has spent years on the job. Inexperienced storm chasers or people who do it just for a thrill make the job more dangerous for professionals like Faidley. They can get in the way and put themselves and others in danger.

"Tornado chasing is 90 percent waiting and 10 percent work," Faidley admits, but it is never dull. "It's so fascinating to have this job where I get up in the morning and just don't know if this is going to be the day that I'm going to get the mother lode of a shot. I like what I'm doing. It's still a lot of fun."

12 **Warren Faidley most likely feels that his job is**

F uneventful.

G dull.

H exciting.

J cautious.

13 **There is enough information in this article to show that**

A television weather reporters are well-informed.

B the government should hire professional storm trackers.

C tornadoes are predictable, if one has the right equipment.

D some people choose a career for its excitement and danger.

14 **You would most likely see a passage like this in**

F a magazine.

G an almanac.

H a novel.

J a dictionary.

15 **In this passage, the word underline{funnel} means**

A a household tool.

B a piece of equipment used to track storms.

C a tornado.

D a type of lightning.

GO

Directions: Choose the best answer for each of the following.

16 <u>Adversity</u> is to <u>prosperity</u> as <u>complication</u> is to

- **F** frustration.
- **G** simplicity.
- **H** acility.
- **J** complexity.

17 <u>Milliliter</u> is to <u>liter</u> as <u>meter</u> is to

- **A** kilometer.
- **B** centimeter.
- **C** millimeter.
- **D** decimeter.

18 <u>Quadruped</u> is to <u>cat</u> as <u>biped</u> is to

- **F** human.
- **G** millipede.
- **H** dog.
- **J** fish.

19 <u>Paris</u> is to <u>France</u> as <u>Rome</u> is to

- **A** England.
- **B** Greece.
- **C** Florence.
- **D** Italy.

Directions: Match words with the same meanings.

20 falter   **F** delight

21 belittle   **G** hesitate

22 revel   **H** disparage

23 concentrate   **J** focus

Directions: Match words with opposite meanings.

24 plentiful   **A** scarce

25 vengeful   **B** forgiving

26 frigid   **C** emotional

27 apathetic   **D** scalding

Directions: Match words with the same meanings.

28 gradual   **F** shared

29 mutual   **G** disastrous

30 prolific   **H** fruitful

31 tragic   **J** step-by-step

STOP

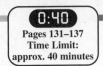

0:40
Pages 131–137
Time Limit:
approx. 40 minutes

Language Arts

Final Test
Language Arts
UNIT **2**

Directions: For Sample A and numbers 1 and 2, read the sentences. Choose the word that correctly completes **both** sentences.

SAMPLE A

Gino _____ tired today.
The soldiers _____ just in time.

A felt
B appeared
C was
D seemed

---

1 Carrie has the _____ to win.

He left us money in his _____.

A will
B drive
C family
D urge

2 My _____ was finished yesterday.

Please _____ to work on time.

F project
G walk
H report
J story

Directions: For numbers 3 and 4, choose the word that means the **opposite** of the underlined word.

3 <u>vacate</u> a building

A empty   C construct
B enter   D design

4 <u>attract</u> insects

F draw   H disturb
G fear   J repel

Directions: For numbers 5 and 6, read the paragraph. For each numbered blank, there is a list of words with the same number. Choose the word from each list that best completes the meaning of the paragraph.

Hawks are in a family of birds called "raptors." They catch and eat small animals, birds, and even fish, and all members of the family are __(5)__ fliers. Raptors can glide on even the slightest breezes. This is why hawks flap their wings so __(6)__.

5 A limited   C incapable
   B superb   D revered

6 F delicately   H infrequently
   G feverishly   J repeatedly

GO

Directions: For numbers 7 and 8, choose the answer that is written correctly and shows the best capitalization and punctuation.

7 **A** Victor said "I take my camera with me everywhere.

B Pia said, "That is the best work we have ever done."

C Alberto said, "that photo on the table is my favorite."

D Marcie claimed, "That she took the best photos."

8 **F** We saw the town's three main attractions: the cathedral, the museum, and the gardens.

G On Saturdays, I like to: eat a big breakfast, and then ride my bike.

H Flying over: Niagara Falls, and the Grand Canyon, was beautiful.

J On our camping trip we saw: rabbits, beavers, and ducks.

Directions: For numbers 9–12, look at the underlined part of the paragraph. Choose the answer that shows the best capitalization and punctuation for that part.

	Dr. Leona Addison
(9)	MicroIndustries
	3242 Main avenue
	Scranton, PA 18523

(10) Dear Dr. Addison

Enclosed is my application for a summer internship. I have heard good things about

(11) your program, and I hope I am accepted. My teacher, Ms. Stone, has already sent you a letter of recommendation.

(12)

Sincerely Yours
Ricky Wolf

9 **A** 3242 Main Avenue

B 3242 Main, avenue

C 3242 main Avenue

D Correct as it is

10 **F** Dear Dr. addison,

G Dear dr. addison,

H Dear Dr. Addison:

J Correct as it is

11 **A** teacher Ms. Stone

B teacher. Ms. Stone

C teacher Ms. Stone,

D Correct as it is

12 **F** sincerely yours

G Sincerely yours,

H Sincerely yours:

J Correct as it is

GO

Directions: For Sample B and numbers 13–16, choose the word that is spelled correctly and best completes the sentence.

SAMPLE B

The late plane caused a lot of _____.

A confuzion
B confusien
C confuseion
D confusion

13 The _____ is stuck.

A doornob   C doorknob
B dorknob   D doorknoob

14 Her performance in the play was _____.

F dramatick   H dramatec
G drumatic   J dramatic

15 He tried to _____ new stamps for his collection.

A akquire   C accuire
B acquire   D aquire

16 They were _____ for the work.

F responsable   H responsibel
G responsabel   J responsible

Directions: For numbers 17–20, read each phrase. Find the underlined word that is not spelled correctly. If all the underlined words are spelled correctly, mark "All correct."

17 A heavily forested
    B customary payment
    C have a remainder
    D loud thunder
    E All correct

18 F serious injury
    G remote teritory
    H save the receipt
    J industrial park
    K All correct

19 A disposable cups
    B strong hurricane
    C horizontle line
    D spread mayonnaise
    E All correct

20 F heavy precipitation
    G specific goals
    H helpful bacteria
    J minimum payment
    K All correct

GO

Directions: For numbers 21–28, mark the answer that shows how the underlined word or phrase should be written correctly.

21 I still have not finished <u>this months report.</u>

  A this month's report.

  B this months report.

  C this months' report.

  D Correct as it is

22 Blanca and Mario packed <u>clothing for they trip.</u>

  F clothing for they's trip.

  G clothing for their trip.

  H clothing for there trip.

  J Correct as it is

23 Pamela is originally from <u>Youngstown; Ohio.</u>

  A Youngstown, Ohio.

  B Youngstown Ohio.

  C youngstown, Ohio

  D Correct as it is

24 <u>'What on Earth is going on.' Marta asked.</u>

  F "What on Earth is going on."

  G "What on Earth is going on?"

  H What on Earth is going on?

  J Correct as it is

25 <u>He and I</u> went to the store.

  A He and me

  B Him, and me

  C Him and I

  D Correct as it is

26 I told Leo <u>I ain't never seen a more fatter cat</u> in my life.

  F I have never seen a more fatter cat

  G I ain't never seen a fatter cat

  H I have never seen a fatter cat

  J Correct as it is

27 I <u>didn't now you weren't</u> ready.

  A did'nt know you were'nt

  B didn't know you weren't

  C didn't now, you were'nt

  D Correct as it is

28 <u>Its almost</u> time to go.

  F Its' almost

  G It's allmost

  H It's almost

  J Correct as it is

GO

Directions: For numbers 29–40, choose the word that is spelled correctly.

29 **A** necessary
   B neccessary
   C neccesary
   D nesessary

30 **F** thorobred
   G thoughroughbred
   H thorobread
   J thoroughbred

31 **A** unbeleiveable
   B unbelieveable
   C unbelevable
   D unbelievable

32 **F** gauge
   G gague
   H gaugue
   J gogue

33 **A** jaundis
   B jondice
   C jaundice
   D johndice

34 **F** repelent
   G reppellent
   H reppelant
   J repellent

35 **A** plateau
   B plateua
   C platau
   D plataeu

36 **F** folage
   G folaige
   H foliage
   J foilage

37 **A** biege
   B beige
   C beighe
   D bieghe

38 **F** airial
   G aireal
   H aeriel
   J aerial

39 **A** hurricane
   B huricane
   C hurracane
   D huricanne

40 **F** refere
   G referee
   H refaree
   J refferee

GO

Directions: For numbers 41–43, choose the word that correctly completes each sentence.

41 **I could tell Ron was pleased with _____ when he finished the test.**

A hisself

B ourself

C itself

D himself

42 **"_____ you watered the plants yet?" Carmella's mother asked.**

F Hasn't

G Haven't

H Didn't

J Has

43 **Mr. Filbert really does _____ those noisy birds of his.**

A loving

B loved

C love

D loves

Directions: For numbers 44 and 45, mark the choice that best combines the sentences.

44 **"You rascal," cried Samantha to the dog. "You stole my peanut butter sandwich!"**

F "You rascal," cried Samantha to the dog, and "You stole my peanut butter sandwich!"

G "You rascal," "You stole my peanut butter sandwich!" Samantha cried to the dog.

H "You rascal," cried Samantha, "You stole my peanut butter sandwich!" to the dog.

J "You rascal," cried Samantha to the dog, "you stole my peanut butter sandwich!"

45 **I did all my homework. I studied. I still thought the test was hard.**

A I did all my homework, I studied, I still thought the test was hard.

B I did all my homework and studied, but I still thought the test was hard.

C I did all my homework; I studied and I still thought the test was hard.

D I did all my homework and I studied and I still thought the test was hard.

GO

Directions: For numbers 46 and 47, choose the sentence that shows correct punctuation and capitalization.

46 **F** Nearly four million people visit the grand canyon every year.

G The canyon and the Colorado river were once considered of little value.

H In 1869 John Wesley Powell led a dangerous expedition down the River in two wooden boats.

J Powell and a few others survived to show the importance of the Colorado and the Grand Canyon.

47 **A** Maxwell Sliffer and his little brother, Simon, are always getting into trouble.

B They love to play practical jokes on people especially on april fool's day.

C One year: they decided to hide their mothers car keys while she was getting ready for work.

D But Mrs sliffer figured out what had happened, and those boys sure were sorry!

Directions: Read the following paragraph and answer numbers 48 and 49.

There are over 300 endangered species in America. One of these is a tiny weasel called the black-footed ferret. Although rarely seen by humans, the black-footed ferret once ranged from Canada to Texas. The prairie dog is the main food of the black-footed ferret. But when the prairie dog was eliminated from farming areas, the black-footed ferret began to disappear.

48 **Which of these would go best after the last sentence in this paragraph?**

F Saving all our endangered species is a goal worth fighting for.

G Wildlife biology is an interesting career, but no one gets rich studying animals.

H The black-footed ferret is a cute little animal, so it's easier to raise money for projects.

J An effort to save the black-footed ferret, therefore, has to include the prairie dog, too.

49 **Which of these sentences would not belong in the paragraph?**

A This little animal was known only to Native Americans for a long time.

B Because few people ever saw a black-footed ferret, no one knew they were almost extinct.

C The smallest group of prairie dogs is called a coterie.

D European settlers didn't see any black-footed ferrets.

STOP

Final Test
Writing

0:30
Pages 138–139
Time Limit:
approx. 30 minutes

Directions: Write a letter to your parents convincing them that you are now old enough to do something they have previously not allowed you to do. Include persuasive reasons why you feel the way you do.

GO

Directions: Write a review of a movie you have seen recently. Would you recommend it to others? Why? Why not? Include information about the movie without revealing the plot.

_____

_____

_____

_____

_____

_____

_____

_____

_____

_____

_____

_____

_____

_____

_____

_____

STOP

Mathematics

SAMPLE A

$6 \times (8 - 3) =$

A 45
B 17
C 30
D 11
E None of these

SAMPLE B

$53.5 \div 0.05 =$

F 107
G 111
H 11
J 1.07
K None of these

---

1 $4.21 \times 0.3 =$

A 1.263
B 12.63
C 126.3
D 1263
E None of these

4 35% of $200 =$

F 1575
G 1.575
H .1575
J 157.5
K None of these

2 $7\frac{1}{8} - 4\frac{5}{6} =$

F $3\frac{7}{24}$
G $2\frac{7}{24}$
H $3\frac{1}{2}$
J $3\frac{17}{24}$
K None of these

5 $\frac{4}{5} \div \frac{1}{2} =$

A $\frac{2}{5}$
B $\frac{5}{8}$
C $1\frac{3}{5}$
D $2\frac{3}{5}$
E None of these

3 $^-36 + 8 =$

A 44
B $^-44$
C 28
D $^-28$
E None of these

6 $^-7 \times {}^-9 =$

F 16
G $^-63$
H $^-2$
J 63
K None of these

GO

Jill's mother bought 5.4 yards of material to make a dress. How could this amount be written as a mixed number?

A $5\frac{1}{4}$

B $5\frac{1}{25}$

C $5\frac{3}{5}$

D $5\frac{4}{10}$

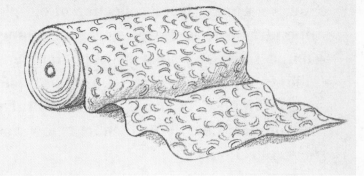

7 **Which of these is another way to write 70,250?**

A $(7 \times 10^4) + (2 \times 10^3) + (5 \times 10^0)$

B $(7 \times 10^4) + (2 \times 10^2) + (5 \times 10^0)$

C $(7 \times 10^4) + (2 \times 10^2) + (5 \times 10^1)$

D $(7 \times 10^3) + (2 \times 10^2) + (5 \times 10^0)$

8 **Which pattern follows this rule?**

Rule: Subtract six tenths.

F 25, 24.4, 23.8, 23.2

G 25, 19, 13, 7

H 25, 24.94, 24.88, 24.82

J 25, 25.6, 26.2, 26.8

GO

Music, Music, Music

9 Stacey's mother has a collection of old phonograph albums as well as a large selection of tapes and compact discs. She has the same number of record albums, tapes, and compact discs as is shown in the chart. Suppose she trades half of her record albums for compact discs. Which chart below would show her new collection?

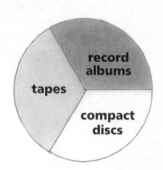

A

B

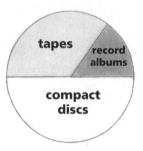

C

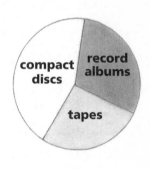

D

10 Jeannie has twice as many compact discs as Stacey has. If *t* represents the number of compact discs Stacey has, what is the number of compact discs Jeannie has?

F $t + 2$ **G** $t - 2$ **H** $t \times 2$ **J** $t \div 2$

11 In Mr. Listo's class, a computer program keeps track of students' scores on a Music Knowledge game. The computer screen shows the scores of five players. Whose score is closest to the mean (average) score of the five players?

A Nancy

B Lisa

C Dave

D Amy

Name	Score
Nancy	28,000
Howie	28,000
Lisa	24,000
Dave	20,000
Amy	18,000

GO

TILING A BATHROOM

12 Milton is tiling his rectangular bathroom floor. He wants to use some triangular tiles, so he will buy square tiles and cut each one in half to form two right triangles. Which of these tiles has been marked to show how he should make his cut?

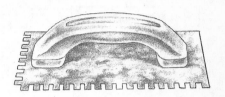

     F   **G**   **H**   **J**

13 Milton paid $19.96 for 4000 milliliters of grout. About how much did he pay per liter?

  A $5.00   **B** $20.00

  C $24.00   **D** $80.00

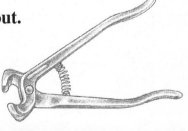

14 This is the pattern with which Milton is tiling the room.

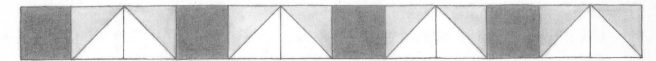

Each pattern is 3 square feet, and 4 repeats of the pattern are shown above. If he uses 60 square feet of tile, how many triangles will there be on the floor?

  F   240   **G**   180

  H   80   **J**   60

GO

15 Each time Bernie writes a number, Arnold divides it by his favorite whole number. Which of these tables could show the results?

Bernie	Arnold
12	17
18	23
21	26

A

Bernie	Arnold
20	14
28	22
37	31

B

Bernie	Arnold
100	25
84	21
16	4

C

Bernie	Arnold
200	600
125	375
39	117

D

16 Margo, Jorge, and Hatsue described the first sign that they saw when they entered the mall.

> Margo said, "The sign has at least one pair of right angles."
> Jorge said, "The sign has at least one obtuse angle."
> Hatsue said, "The sign has exactly one pair of parallel sides."

Which of these is the sign they describe?

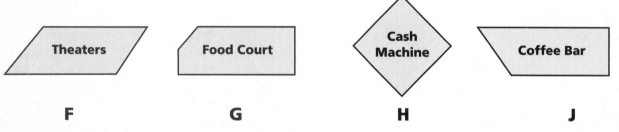

Theaters **F**   Food Court **G**   Cash Machine **H**   Coffee Bar **J**

17 The numbers in the square are all multiples of a certain whole number greater than 1. Which of these numbers is also a multiple of that number?

A 11
B 13
C 29
D 56

14	**84**
63	
	49

GO

Directions: Choose the correct answer for numbers 18–23.

18
407
×265

F 34,595
G 107,855
H 108,755
J 836,455

19 2.7) 0.54

A 0.002
B 0.02
C 0.2
D 2.2

20 0.4 × 375.23 =

F 15.0092
G 150.092
H 151.092
J 170.092

21
$\frac{4}{5}$
$-\frac{1}{5}$

A $4\frac{1}{5}$
B $\frac{3}{5}$
C $\frac{4}{25}$
D $\frac{1}{4}$

22 What is 2.19 rounded to the nearest tenth?

F 2.210
G 2.20
H 2.10
J 2.01

23 Leonard bought a pair of running shoes on sale for $48. The regular price of the shoes is $60. What percentage discount is this?

A 20%
B 18%
C 12%
D 1.2%

Directions: Choose the correct answer for numbers 24–29.

24 Sally bought this refrigerator when she went away to college. What is the volume of the refrigerator?

F 4 cu ft.

G 6.5 cu ft.

H 7.5 cu ft.

J 9 cu ft.

25 Which statement about this triangle is true?

A Only one of the angles is an acute angle.

B Two of the angles are obtuse angles.

C There is one right and one acute angle.

D None of the angles are right angles.

26 Tomas arrived at the museum at 9:15 and left $2\frac{1}{2}$ hours later. At what time did he leave the museum?

F 11:15

G 11:30

H 11:45

J 12:30

27 What is the square root of 169?

A 1

B 12

C 13

D 28,561

28 What time does the clock show?

F 9:50

G 9:53

H 10:49

J 10:50

29 122 millimeters =

A 1.22 meters

B 12.2 decimeters

C 1.22 kilometers

D 12.2 centimeters

GO

Directions: Choose the correct answer for numbers 30– 35.

30 **What value of *x* makes this sentence true?**

$721 + (482 + 593) = (721 + 482) + x$

F 1203
G 1075
H 593
J 482

31 **The expression |⁻36| represents**

A 6.
B ⁻6.
C 36.
D ⁻36.

32 **A recipe for trail mix calls for 8 ounces of cereal, 3 ounces of dried fruit, and 5 ounces of nuts. About what fraction of the trail mix is cereal?**

F $\frac{1}{8}$
G $\frac{1}{2}$
H $\frac{1}{3}$
J $\frac{3}{14}$

33 **Which of these is the largest fraction?**

A $\frac{2}{5}$
B $\frac{2}{7}$
C $\frac{2}{3}$
D $\frac{2}{9}$

34 **The length of a sofa would be closest to**

F 6 feet.
G 10 inches.
H 2 feet.
J 5 yards.

35 **In an 8-hour time period, 160 cars cross a bridge. On average, how many cars crossed the bridge each hour?**

A 20
B 28
C 30
D 168

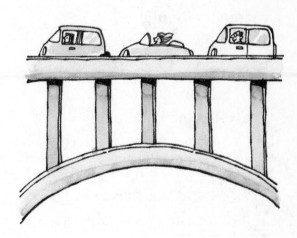

GO

Directions: Choose the correct answer for numbers 36 –41.

36 You know the measurements of two angles in a triangle. They are 39 degrees and 84 degrees. What is the measurement of the third angle?

F 180 degrees

G 123 degrees

H 57 degrees

J None of the above

37 Kelly's class wants to hold a carnival. They have saved $1500 to host it. They will need $750 for equipment, $329 for food and beverages, and $192 to have posters and tickets made. How much money will they need to buy prizes for carnival attendants?

A $1271

B $239

C $229

D Not enough information

38 Two numbers have a product of 119,784 and a difference of 1870. What are the two numbers?

F 2791 and 921

G 3864 and 31

H 1932 and 62

J 1496 and 394

39 A triangle is 27.2 centimeters high and 36 centimeters wide at its base. What is the area of the triangle?

A 979.2 square centimeters

B 489.6 square centimeters

C 73.2 square centimeters

D Not enough information

40 Stuey is doing a 10-mile walk for charity. Each of his sponsors promises to pay him $1 for every mile that he walks. If he finishes the walk, how much money will he earn for charity?

F $10

G $100

H $1000

J Not enough information

41 Which one of these number sentences is false?

A $\frac{1}{2} > \frac{1}{4}$

B $0.0136 > 0.13$

C $\frac{1}{4} = 0.25$

D $10.56 > 1.056$

STOP

Pages 149 – 150
Time Limit:
approx. 15 minutes

Social Studies

Final Test
Social Studies  UNIT 4

Directions: For numbers 1 and 2, look at the map and answer the questions that follow.

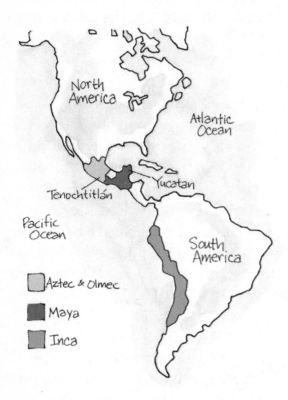

1 **Where was the Mayan civilization located?**

A in South America

B on the Yucatan Peninsula

C on the Pacific coast

D near the Amazon River

2 **Where were the Aztec and Olmec civilizations?**

F in the Plains states

G in Cuzco

H near Tenochtitlán

J on an island

Directions: For numbers 3 –5, choose the correct answer.

3 **During the Scientific Movement, who began analytic geometry?**

A René Descartes

B Leonardo da Vinci

C Galen

D John Locke

4 **Galileo was brought before the Inquisition because**

F he had split from the Church to form his own religion.

G he had stated that planets move.

H he had discovered America.

J he had offended his family members.

5 **Doctors did all of the following before the eighteenth century except**

A study blood circulation.

B draw the human body.

C take x-rays.

D create an antibiotic ointment.

GO

Directions: For numbers 6–9, read the passage and answer the questions that follow.

Feudal Society

Safety was a serious concern during the Middle Ages. Many people chose to form small communities. These communities revolved around the lord, also known as the *master*. The communities' roots tracked back to Germanic tribes. In these tribes, the warriors engaged in battle for the chief, and in turn, the chief took care of the things the warriors needed.

The structure of feudal society looked much like a pyramid. The king was at the top of the pyramid and peasants were at the bottom. The king gave land grants, also known as *fiefs*, to lords. In exchange, the lords provided soldiers for the king. The lord provided fiefs to lesser lords, also known as *vassals*. The vassals lived on and worked the land. The lord owned the land. When the vassal died, the right to live on and work the land passed from the vassal to the vassal's living relatives.

Feudal life was based on the feudal contract, a set of rules. Not all of the rules were written, but people were familiar with them because of local customs. Vassals were protected by the lord. He held court to resolve disagreements. If a vassal died, the lord cared for the vassal's children. In exchange, vassals paid money and gave military service to the lord.

6 **Which of the following statements about feudal society is not true?**

F Feudal society was based on Germanic tribes.

G Military service and land were given in exchange for a fief.

H A feudal lord acted as a court judge to resolve disagreements.

J A lord passed ownership of the fief to a vassal's relatives when the vassal died.

7 **Another term for *fief* is**

A lesser lord.   **C** land grant.

B tribe.   **D** peasant.

8 **A king during the time of feudal society was most like which person in a company today?**

F president

G vice president

H secretary

J assistant

9 **From the information in the passage, you can tell that there were more _____ than _____.**

A kings than peasants

B vassals than lords

C lords than peasants

D fiefs than vassals

STOP

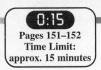

Pages 151–152
Time Limit:
approx. 15 minutes

Science

Directions: For numbers 1–6, choose the correct answer.

1 **Which of the following is the best definition for *data*?**

A numbers gathered from an experiment or project

B ideas

C facts

D an educated guess about what will happen in an experiment or project

2 **The mass of an element or compound sample is most likely to be expressed in**

F milliliters.

G kilometers.

H degrees.

J grams.

3 **This is not part of the human digestive system.**

A the colon

B the stomach

C the small intestine

D the lungs

4 **The best example of a way to conserve natural resources is**

F regulating toxic emissions from cars.

G the greenhouse effect.

H cutting down on packaging used in consumer goods.

J keeping garbage dumps away from residential areas.

5 **The force that is most likely to cause an object to fall from a table is**

A density.

B gravity.

C acceleration.

D velocity.

6 **Plants _____ their own food through the process of photosynthesis.**

F decompose

G consume

H chlorophyll

J produce

Science

Directions: Read the passage. Then choose the best answer to numbers 7–10.

Vital Volcanoes

When you picture a volcano in your mind, you probably think of a giant, quaking mountain that breathes fire and spews destruction. Fast-flowing lava has been known to claim lives and damage personal property. Clouds of toxic gas and hot ash have also created a range of problems, from acid rain to structural damage, agricultural devastation to human suffocation. To make matters worse, volcanic activity is often accompanied by earthquakes and tsunamis.

What you may not know, however, is that volcanic eruptions play a vital role in the Earth's life cycle. The island of Hawaii, for example, was created by volcanic activity in the Pacific Ocean. Volcanic eruptions create fertile soil, so the island is well-suited to lush, green growth. In addition, corals naturally grow on the slopes of new volcanoes.

In addition to forming new islands, volcanoes create deposits of valuable minerals such as silver and gold, as well as renewable geothermal energy that can be harnessed and used to generate electricity and heat.

7 **Which of the following is not a harmful side effect of volcanic eruptions?**

A lava flows

B gas clouds

C gold deposits

D all of the above

8 **Geothermal energy is renewable. This means that**

F if your house is heated with geothermal energy, you can pay to get more of it.

G it cannot be permanently diminished.

H it can create electricity and heat.

J it can be diminished.

9 **Why are volcanic eruptions good for crops?**

A Clouds of toxic gas create agricultural devastation.

B They create fertile soil.

C They create geothermal energy.

D Volcanic eruptions destroy homes to make more room for crops.

10 **The author of this passage is trying to**

F inform you about how volcanoes can be helpful and harmful.

G persuade you to visit Volcano National Park in Hawaii.

H tell you a funny story about volcanoes.

J inform you how to harness geothermal energy.

STOP

Grade 7 Answer Key

Page 26
1. B
2. F
3. C
4. G
5. A
6. J

Page 28
1. B
2. H
3. A
4. J
5. B
6. F
7. A
8. G
9. D
10. F

Page 30
1. A
2. B
3. A
4. B
5. B
6. A
7. B
8. A
9. B
10. B
11. B
12. A

Page 32
1. D
2. A
3. B
4. C
5. G
6. H
7. J
8. F
9. C
10. A
11. D
12. B
13. H
14. J
15. F
16. G

Page 34
1. C
2. F
3. B
4. J
5. D
6. H
7. B
8. F
9. B
10. F

Page 36

FIRST QUESTION: Possible response: The author wanted to inform me about Leadbelly. I know this because of the many facts that are included in the passage.

SECOND QUESTION: Born in 1888, Huddie Ledbetter, nicknamed "Leadbelly," was a blues guitarist who inspired generations of musicians.

THIRD QUESTION: The turning point in Leadbelly's career was in 1934 when he was "discovered." This was a turning point because he then found a much larger audience for his music.

FOURTH QUESTION: Possible response: Leadbelly's musical style influenced many musicians.

Page 38
1. C
2. G
3. C
4. H
5. C

Page 41
1. A
2. J
3. B
4. J
5. C
6. H

Grade 7 Answer Key

Page 42
7. B
8. J
9. A
10. J

Page 44
Responses will vary.

Page 46
1. A
2. F
3. D
4. G

Page 48
1. C
2. F
3. C
4. G
5. C
6. H

Page 50
1. $21.00
2. $25.60
3. 45 points
4. 4 tattoos
5. 24 nickels

Page 52
1. B
2. G
3. A
4. F
5. C
6. J

Page 54
1. C
2. F
3. D
4. J
5. C
6. G

Page 56
1. A
2. J
3. D
4. F
5. D
6. G

Page 58
1. D
2. G
3. A
4. H
5. B
6. G
7. D
8. H

Page 60
1. B
2. F
3. C
4. G
5. D
6. F
7. B
8. F

Page 62
1. D
2. F
3. D
4. G
5. C
6. F

Page 64
1. C
2. J
3. A
4. H
5. A

Page 68
1. B
2. F
3. B
4. G
5. D

Page 69
6. H
7. B
8. J

Page 72
1. C
2. J
3. A
4. J
5. C
6. H

Page 79
A. D
B. G

Page 82
1. D
2. G
3. C
4. G
5. A
6. G

Page 83
7. B
8. J
9. A
10. J

Page 85
11. D
12. G
13. A
14. H
15. B

Grade 7 Answer Key

Page 86
16. G
17. A
18. J
19. D
20. F
21. A

Page 87
22. H
23. D

Page 88
C. A

Page 89
24. B
25. J

Page 90
26. C
27. F
28. B
29. J
30. A
31. J

Page 91
D. D
32. B
33. H

Page 92
34. A
35. J

Page 93
36. B
37. H
38. D

Page 94
A. C
1. B
2. J
B. F
3. C
4. J

Page 95
5. C
6. H
7. A
8. G
9. B
10. F
11. C
12. J

Page 96
C. B
13. C
14. G
15. D
16. H

Page 97
17. A
18. H
19. C
20. J
21. B
22. F

Page 98
D. E
23. B
24. J
25. A
26. H
27. E

Page 99
FIRST QUESTION: Responses will vary, but should reflect that Alex is the main character.

SECOND QUESTION: The conflict is that Alex must take care of Connie, but the two do not get along.

THIRD QUESTION: Alex wants to be in charge of Connie all the time, but you can tell that she loves her because she holds Connie when they are scared and snuggles with her when they sleep.

Page 100
Responses will vary.

Grade 7 Answer Key

Page 101
E. B
28. D
29. F
30. B
31. J
32. A
33. H

Page 102
34. D
35. H
36. C
37. F
38. D
39. G

Page 103
40. A
41. H
42. C
43. J
F. E
44. B
45. K
46. A
47. J

Page 104
Responses
will vary.

Page 105
A. B
B. K
1. D
2. F
3. C
4. J

Page 106
C. B

Page 107
5. A
6. J
7. A

Page 108
8. H
9. D
10. G
11. B
12. J

Page 109
13. C
14. H

Page 110
15. C
16. J
17. B
18. F

Page 111
D. A
E. H
19. C
20. K
21. A
22. K
23. B
24. J

Page 112
F. D
25. D
26. F

Page 113
27. E
28. F
29. C
30. G

Page 114
31. C
32. H
33. D

Page 115
1. B
2. H
3. D
4. G
5. B
6. G
7. C
8. J

Page 116
9. C
10. F
11. A
12. G
13. C
14. G
15. A

Page 117
16. H
17. A
18. J

Page 118
19. B
20. H
21. A
22. J

Page 119
1. C
2. G

Page 120
3. C
4. G
5. A
6. H
7. D

Grade 7 Answer Key

Page 121
8. F
9. D
10. F
11. C
12. F
13. C
14. G
15. C

Page 122
16. J
17. B
18. H
19. B
20. F

Page 125
A. B

Page 126
1. C
2. G
3. B
4. J
5. A

Page 127
6. H
7. A
8. J
9. A

Page 128
10. G
11. B

Page 129
12. H
13. D
14. F
15. C

Page 130
16. G
17. A
18. F
19. D
20. G
21. H
22. F
23. J
24. A
25. B
26. D
27. C
28. J
29. F
30. H
31. G

Page 131
A. B
1. A
2. H
3. B
4. J
5. B
6. H

Page 132
7. B
8. F
9. A
10. H
11. D
12. G

Page 133
B. D
13. C
14. J
15. B
16. J
17. E
18. G
19. C
20. K

Page 134
21. A
22. G
23. A
24. G
25. D
26. H
27. B
28. H

Page 135
29. A
30. J
31. D
32. F
33. C
34. J
35. A
36. H
37. B
38. J
39. A
40. G

Page 136
41. D
42. G
43. C
44. J
45. B

Page 137
46. J
47. A
48. J
49. C

Page 138
Responses will vary.

Page 139
Responses will vary.

Grade 7 Answer Key

Page 140

A. C
B. K
1. A
2. G
3. D
4. K
5. C
6. J

Page 141

C. D
7. C
8. F

Page 142

9. C
10. H
11. B

Page 143

12. F
13. A
14. H

Page 144

15. C
16. J
17. D

Page 145

18. G
19. C
20. G
21. B
22. G
23. A

page 146

24. J
25. D
26. H
27. C
28. H
29. D

Page 147

30. H
31. C
32. G
33. C
34. F
35. A

Page 148

36. H
37. D
38. H
39. B
40. J
41. B

Page 149

1. B
2. H
3. A
4. G
5. C

Page 150

6. G
7. C
8. F
9. B

Page 151

1. C
2. J
3. D
4. H
5. B
6. J

Page 152

7. C
8. G
9. B
10. F

McGraw-Hill Children's Publishing

All our workbooks meet school curriculum guidelines and correspond to
The McGraw-Hill Companies classroom textbooks.

SPECTRUM SERIES

SPECTRUM WORKBOOKS FEATURING MERCER MAYER'S LITTLE CRITTER®
GRADES K–2

The nation's premier educational publisher for grades K–12, together with the well-known Mercer Mayer's Little Critter® characters, represents a collaboration of two highly respected "institutions" in the fields of education and children's literature. Like other Spectrum titles, the length, breadth and depth of the activities in these workbooks enable children to learn a variety of skills about a single subject.

- Mercer Mayer's Little Critter family of characters has sold over 100 million books. These wholesome characters and stories appeal to both parents and teachers.
- These entertaining books are based on highly respected McGraw-Hill Companies' textbooks.
- Each book includes easy-to-follow instructions.
- Page counts range from 128–160 full-color pages.
- An answer key is included in each book.

NEW!
Spelling, Writing, and Language Arts for Grades K–2

TITLE	ISBN	PRICE
Gr. K - Math	1-57768-800-7	$7.95
Gr. 1 - Math	1-57768-801-5	$7.95
Gr. 2 - Math	1-57768-802-3	$7.95
Gr. K - Reading	1-57768-810-4	$7.95
Gr. 1 - Reading	1-57768-811-2	$7.95
Gr. 2 - Reading	1-57768-812-0	$7.95
Gr. K - Phonics	1-57768-820-1	$7.95
Gr. 1 - Phonics	1-57768-821-X	$7.95
Gr. 2 - Phonics	1-57768-822-8	$7.95
NEW Gr. K - Spelling	1-57768-830-9	$7.95
NEW Gr. 1 - Spelling	1-57768-831-7	$7.95
NEW Gr. 2 - Spelling	1-57768-832-5	$7.95
NEW Gr. K - Writing	1-57768-850-3	$7.95
NEW Gr. 1 - Writing	1-57768-851-1	$7.95
NEW Gr. 2 - Writing	1-57768-852-X	$7.95
NEW Gr. K - Language Arts	1-57768-840-6	$7.95
NEW Gr. 1 - Language Arts	1-57768-841-4	$7.95
NEW Gr. 2 - Language Arts	1-57768-842-2	$7.95

Prices subject to change without notice.

MATH
GRADES K–8

This series features easy-to-follow instructions that give students a clear path to success. This series includes comprehensive coverage of the basic skills, helping children master math fundamentals. Most titles have more than 150 full-color pages, including an answer key.

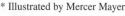

TITLE	ISBN	PRICE
Gr. K - Math *	1-57768-800-7	$7.95
Gr. 1 - Math *	1-57768-801-5	$7.95
Gr. 2 - Math *	1-57768-802-3	$7.95
Gr. 3 - Math	1-57768-403-6	$7.95
Gr. 4 - Math	1-57768-404-4	$7.95
Gr. 5 - Math	1-57768-405-2	$7.95
Gr. 6 - Math	1-57768-406-0	$7.95
Gr. 7 - Math	1-57768-407-9	$7.95
Gr. 8 - Math	1-57768-408-7	$7.95

* Illustrated by Mercer Mayer

READING
GRADES K–6

This full-color series creates an enjoyable reading environment, even for those who find reading challenging. Each book contains interesting content and colorful, compelling illustrations, so children are eager to find out what happens next. Most titles have more than 150 pages, including an answer key.

TITLE	ISBN	PRICE
Gr. K - Reading *	1-57768-810-4	$7.95
Gr. 1 - Reading *	1-57768-811-2	$7.95
Gr. 2 - Reading *	1-57768-812-0	$7.95
Gr. 3 - Reading	1-57768-463-X	$7.95
Gr. 4 - Reading	1-57768-464-8	$7.95
Gr. 5 - Reading	1-57768-465-6	$7.95
Gr. 6 - Reading	1-57768-466-4	$7.95

* Illustrated by Mercer Mayer

PHONICS/WORD STUDY
GRADES K–6

The books in this series provide everything children need to build multiple skills in language. Focusing on phonics, structural analysis, and dictionary skills, this series also offers creative ideas for using phonics and word study skills in language arts. Most titles have more than 200 pages, including an answer key.

TITLE	ISBN	PRICE
Gr. K - Phonics *	1-57768-820-1	$7.95
Gr. 1 - Phonics *	1-57768-821-X	$7.95
Gr. 2 - Phonics *	1-57768-822-8	$7.95
Gr. 3 - Phonics	1-57768-453-2	$7.95
Gr. 4 - Word Study & Phonics	1-57768-454-0	$7.95
Gr. 5 - Word Study & Phonics	1-57768-455-9	$7.95
Gr. 6 - Word Study & Phonics	1-57768-456-7	$7.95

* Illustrated by Mercer Mayer

SPELLING
GRADES K–6

This full-color series links spelling to reading and writing and increases skills in words and meanings, consonant and vowel spellings, and proofreading practice. Over 200 pages. Speller dictionary and answer key included.

TITLE	ISBN	PRICE
Gr. K - Spelling *	1-57768-830-9	$7.95
Gr. 1 - Spelling *	1-57768-831-7	$7.95
Gr. 2 - Spelling *	1-57768-832-5	$7.95
Gr. 3 - Spelling	1-57768-493-1	$7.95
Gr. 4 - Spelling	1-57768-494-X	$7.95
Gr. 5 - Spelling	1-57768-495-8	$7.95
Gr. 6 - Spelling	1-57768-496-6	$7.95

* Illustrated by Mercer Mayer

LANGUAGE ARTS
GRADES K–6

Encourages creativity and builds confidence by making writing fun! Seventy-two four-part lessons strengthen writing skills by focusing on parts of speech, word usage, sentence structure, punctuation, and proofreading. Each level includes a Writer's Handbook at the end of the book that offers writing tips. This series is based on the highly respected SRA/McGraw-Hill language arts series. More than 180 full-color pages.

TITLE	ISBN	PRICE
Gr. K - Language Arts *	1-57768-840-6	$7.95
Gr. 1 - Language Arts *	1-57768-841-4	$7.95
Gr. 2 - Language Arts *	1-57768-842-2	$7.95
Gr. 3 - Language Arts	1-57768-483-4	$7.95
Gr. 4 - Language Arts	1-57768-484-2	$7.95
Gr. 5 - Language Arts	1-57768-485-0	$7.95
Gr. 6 - Language Arts	1-57768-486-9	$7.95

* Illustrated by Mercer Mayer

WRITING
GRADES K–6

Lessons focus on creative and expository writing using clearly stated objectives and pre-writing exercises. Eight essential reading skills are applied. Activities include main idea, sequence, comparison, detail, fact and opinion, cause and effect, and making a point. Over 130 pages. Answer key included.

TITLE	ISBN	PRICE
Gr. K - Writing *	1-57768-850-3	$7.95
Gr. 1 - Writing *	1-57768-851-1	$7.95
Gr. 2 - Writing *	1-57768-852-X	$7.95
Gr. 3 - Writing	1-57768-913-5	$7.95
Gr. 4 - Writing	1-57768-914-3	$7.95
Gr. 5 - Writing	1-57768-915-1	$7.95
Gr. 6 - Writing	1-57768-916-X	$7.95

* Illustrated by Mercer Mayer

Prices subject to change without notice.